REMEMBER WHEN —

Trolley Wires Spanned the Country

REMEMBER WHEN —

Trolley Wires Spanned the Country

Bulletin 119 of Central Electric Railfans' Association

Norman Carlson and Arthur Peterson Co-Editors

Issued in commemoration of the Fortieth
Anniversary of Central Electric Railfans' Association
1938-1978

REMEMBER WHEN —
Trolley Wires Spanned the Country

Bulletin 119 of Central Electric Railfans' Association

Copyright© 1980
by Central Electric Railfans' Association
All rights reserved
An Illinois Not-for-profit Corporation
Post Office Box 503 Chicago, Illinois 60690 U.S.A.

Library of Congress Catalog Card No. 78-74495
International Standard Book Number 0-915348-20-9

CO-EDITORS
NORMAN CARLSON   ARTHUR PETERSON

EDITORIAL STAFF
RICHARD N. LUKIN   ANTHONY J. SCHILL

CONTRIBUTORS

Charles A. Brown	Raymond F. Corley	John E. Koschwanez	William D. Middleton
Frank E. Butts	Donald Duke	George Krambles	William E. Robertson
Joseph M. Canfield	Frank B. Fairbanks	Gordon E. Lloyd	J. Schmit
Norton D. Clark	Truman Hefner	Robert T. McVay	James P. Shuman
David H. Cope	William C. Janssen	Robert V. Mehlenbeck	John D. Siebert

CERA Bulletins are technical, educational references prepared as historical projects by members of Central Electric Railfans' Association, working without salary due to their interest in the subject. This Bulletin is consistent with the stated purpose of the corporation: To foster the study of the history, equipment and operation of electric railways. If you the reader can provide any unknown information or are of the opinion that certain information is incorrect please send your information, documented by source material where possible to: Curator of Corrections, Central Electric Railfans' Association, P.O. Box 503, Chicago, Illinois 60690, U.S.A.

REMEMBER WHEN — Trolley Wires Spanned the Country was designed by Norman Carlson. Color Separations and assembly are by Jim Walter Graphic Arts of Beloit, Wisconsin with typesetting by Guetschow Typesetting of South Beloit, Illinois. The dustcover is designed by Quicksilver of Chicago, Illinois. The book was printed by Sorg Printing Company of Chicago, Illinois and was bound by John F. Cuneo Company, Melrose Park, Illinois.

ACKNOWLEDGMENT

We wish to acknowledge the assistance of several people without whom this book would never have existed. First, to each of the contributors, for generously sharing their fine photographic works and for help in generating caption material. Jim Walter nursed this project along, providing significant technical guidance as well as arranging for production details when your editors could not spare any more time from their professional responsibilities. Individual photographers are of course credited at each caption.

We should also mention the efforts of James J. Buckley and Dr. Harold E. Cox, who assisted with roster and operational data, and the help of Charles J. Dengler, Arthur D. Dubin, Arthur S. Ellis, Francis J. Goldsmith, John F. Humiston, LeRoy O. King, Jr., John D. Knowles, John McKane, J. Andrew Sack, Fred Schneider and Bernard L. Stone for assistance with the particularly vexing properties, locations and editorial development. Dick Lukin and Tony Schill provided much assistance in reading drafts of captions and recommending editorial changes. Perhaps above all we owe a debt of gratitude to the dreamers, designers, builders, financers and operators without whom the subjects of this album could never have existed.

Finally, special thanks are due to Louise and Ann Williams for making the electric railway items from the library of Allan C. Williams available to the editors, Evelyn Carlson for her editorial suggestions and assistance, Anna Weber for typing seemingly endless revisions of captions and Kathleen Carlson, not only for her patience, but for assisting with editorial development of captions.

Norman Carlson

Arthur Peterson

Chicago, Illinois
September, 1980

INTRODUCTION

Be it a local streetcar, a high-speed interurban or an electrified mainline railroad, the overhead wire that delivered electricity from the central generating station to the streetcar or train was the trolley wire. At one time, trolley wire was suspended over countless miles of streetcar tracks, almost 15,500 miles of interurban railways and 2,800 route-miles of electrified mainline railroads. Technically, the trolley wire is a hard-drawn, grooved copper wire that is typically suspended from transverse span wires or bracket arms strung from poles alongside the tracks. But whatever the technical description, the trolley in its popular usage described the means of travel to family, friends and business associates alike. This album of photographs is presented so that each of us may recall the electric railways that once crossed the country. We have documented the contribution that these railways made to our society to commemorate forty years of work by our organization, Central Electric Railfans' Association.

The history of Central Electric Railfans' Association dates from the 1930's. In the early 1930's, there were very few people interested in electric railways other than as a means of transportation. For those who had special interests, the only means of communication were advertisements in *Railroad Magazine*, offering to exchange trolley pictures. George Krambles of Chicago and James P. Shuman of Lancaster, Pennsylvania, were two such people placing ads. One of George's ads was read by Robert V. Mehlenbeck of Peoria, Illinois, who was astounded to find someone else interested in trolleys. Bob, who was saving every last penny for film, told his friend William C. Janssen about this George Krambles of Chicago. Bob wrote to George and started to trade pictures. Meanwhile, Bill was saving his every last penny to ride streetcars and interurbans. Late in 1932, George journeyed to Peoria to meet Bob and Bill, and the friendship grew. Later George and Bill were roommates at the University of Illinois, where they met Barney Stone and Earle Thompson.

Meanwhile, interest in electric railways on the East Coast was not limited to Jim Shuman, as other organizations were being formed. E. Jay Quinby initiated the electric Railroaders' Association in New York City during 1934. Its purpose is to document and preserve the history of electric railways. Jim Shuman was instrumental in the formation of the National Railway Historical Society, an organization, based in Philadelphia, whose purpose is to document and preserve the history of railroads in general. Both of these organizations, like CERA, continue their activities in 1978.

Back in Chicago, another individual, Ray Colombe, was moving forward in organizing the Railroad Club of Chicago. At this time still another organization, the Railroad Boosters, was being managed by Wayne and Ralph Melching, the Eichstaedt brothers and Earle Thompson. The Railroad Boosters had a mimeograph publication edited and produced by George Krambles. An interesting adjunct to this newsletter were small individual photographs printed by Bob Mehlenbeck and pasted onto the mimeo paper. The large circulation list of the newsletter was testimony to the magnitude of this effort.

Independent of these groups, Frank Butts continued his interest in electric railways. In 1937, he rode a NRHS fantrip on the Toledo, Port Clinton & Lakeside. Frank thought that similar trips would be most desirable in the Chicago area, and that the Gary Railways would be an interesting line to ride. Consequently, Frank had placed an advertisement, with a conveniently assumed name for an organization which did not then exist, in the "Coming Fan Excursions" column on page 33 of the April 1938, issue of *Railroad Magazine,* which said:

> Out of Gary, Ind., about April 10 . . .
> The Electric Railroaders' Association in Chicago is planning a jaunt over the Gary-Valparaiso line of the Gary Rys., to include 100 miles of travel, part of trip over right-of-way and track of the defunct New York-Chicago Air Line, etc. Fare will be about $1; address Frank E. Butts, 1118 East 64th Street, Chicago, Ill., before April first.

After reading this advertisement, George Krambles and Barney Stone journeyed to the Woodlawn area of Chicago to meet Frank Butts. At this meeting George and Barney offered to help Frank with his proposed trip, which was ultimately scheduled for May 1st.

On May 1, 1938, 75 people rode over Gary Railways between Gary and Valparaiso, Indiana, in response to Frank's ad. Six weeks later, on June 19, 1938, 180 people rode a six-car train of Shore Line route equipment over the entire interurban system of the Chicago, North Shore & Milwaukee Railroad. The success of these trips prompted consideration of forming an organization. In the August 1940, issue of *Mass Transportation,* George Krambles described how the name of the organization was selected:

> In a conference one sultry afternoon in early July 1938, the name of the new group was selected from twenty proposed and we believe the term *Railfan* was coined to meet our requirements; at least, it was independently arrived at and adopted into the new club's name: *Central Electric Railfans' Association.*

On October 14, 1938, the inaugural meeting of CERA was held. There were 40 persons in attendance. This meeting was arranged with the cooperation of the Chicago, South Shore & South Bend Railroad, who made available a passenger car in Randolph Street terminal. The agenda included not only organization of the association, but movies of Texas interurbans as well.

In those early years, CERA was the beneficiary of the friendly rivalry between J. M. Michaels, Passenger Traffic Manager, North Shore Line, and R. E. Jamieson, Passenger Traffic Manager, South Shore Line. Joe Michaels was CERA's first corporate "sponsor." It was through his efforts that the six-car fantrip was operated in June, 1938. However, "Jamie" was not to be outclassed by that upstart to the north. So for CERA Trip number 9, on June 25, 1939, the South Shore assembled a six-car train that consisted of a combine, three coaches, a 12-wheeled parlor car on the rear and coach 35, which had its regular seating removed and was equipped as a lunch counter car *for that day only.*

From a base of its founding members, George Krambles (member number 1), Bernard L. Stone (2), Frank E. Butts (3), Albert C. Kalmbach (4), John F. Humiston (5), Earle R. Thompson (6), John K. Hrdina (7), Joseph M. Michaels (8), Theodore A. Kawol (9), William C. Janssen (10), and Robert V. Mehlenbeck (11), CERA has continually developed. (By press-time of this Bulletin, member number 4,700 has been registered in CERA!)

CERA Bulletins originated as a "pass-out" on fantrips. They were intended to be a record of the trip, containing a brief history and other interesting facts concerning the railway the group was riding. Monthly meetings were also held in electric railway cars, but perhaps the most fondly remembered were the "Dinner in the Diner" meetings. The North Shore Line would set out dining car 409 and a coach on track 4 at the Wilson Avenue "L" station, (then not a main line but a stub track). Following dinner, the group would adjourn to the coach for the scheduled program. This tradition of dining car sessions continues 40 years later, with our annual "dining car" trip on the South Shore Line. Although the menu is not as sumptuous, the buffet dinner in South Shore's party car continues the tradition.

Forty years later, CERA has held approximately 350 meetings, issued 118 Bulletins and operated 148 fantrips. The organization has nearly 2,000 active currently. The management of the organization has passed to the "second and third" generations; however, the advice and counsel of the founding members is eagerly sought and willingly given.

The strength of the organization is attested by the fact that founding members Krambles, Stone, Butts, Humiston and Mehlenbeck, together with Jim Shuman and many other early members attended the 40th Anniversary banquet in Chicago on May 27, 1978. And, as you can read in the acknowledgments and contributors to this Bulletin, this group of people was also instrumental in the publication of this commemorative album. With the continued participation of these members and many of those who followed, the future of CERA looks brighter with each passing day.

As we enter the 1980's, we hope that this album will not only revitalize memories of our senior members, but will also acquaint younger people to the extent of electric railway services once provided in the United States. In 1980, the increasing cost of petroleum and concern for the environment is creating new interest in urban as well as mainline electric rail facilities. Renewal and expansion is underway in Chicago, Boston, Cleveland, Philadelphia, Pittsburgh, New York, Toronto, Montreal and San Francisco. New systems are under construction in Atlanta, Baltimore, Buffalo, Calgary, Edmonton, Miami, San Diego and Washington, D.C., while Los Angeles, Detroit and Portland seem certain to start building electrified rail systems very soon. Not since the early days of the century has the future of the industry looked brighter. Thus, it is with considerable optimism that we present CERA Bulletin 119, *Remember When — Trolley Wires Spanned the Country.*

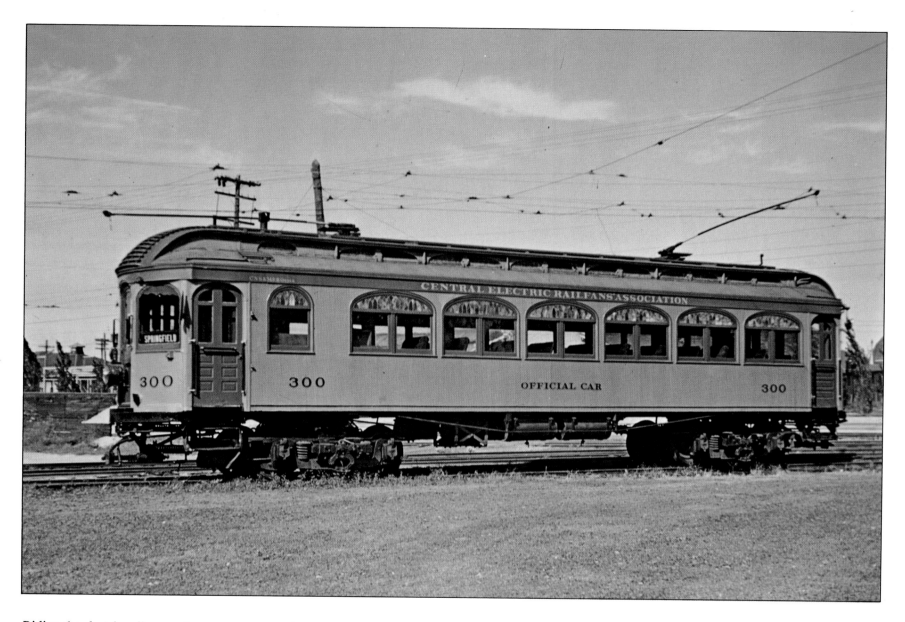

Riding the electric railways of yesteryear was a pleasure to some and drudgery to others. Among the people who recall those rides with pleasure are members of Central Electric Railfans' Association. Most memorable were the trips on the Chicago North Shore & Milwaukee in CERA "Official Club Car" 300. In 1939, the North Shore Line provided the car's exclusive use in exchange for maintaining the car. The individualism of the restoration is evidenced by the various styles of car numbers. Later, window curtains and other interior amenities followed. Until World War II, car 300 was used as a gathering place to swap stories and photographs and to display souvenirs. To assist in recalling your personal memories, we are pleased to present this photographic album of a trip around the United States and Canada in the twenty years following 1938. — *Charles A. Brown*

Our mythical trip on electric railways in the United States, Canada and Cuba that operated during CERA's existence begins on the world's largest street railway, Chicago Surface Lines. In its waning years of service, "Big Pullman" 532 leaves the Milwaukee/Imlay loop. On this beautiful day in 1948, the car will travel from the extreme northwest corner of the city to downtown along Milwaukee Avenue, a street that is a symbol of the city itself. Unfortunately, many of the scenes portrayed in this album are now only memories. For instance, buses replaced streetcars on Milwaukee Avenue in 1952, car 532 was scrapped in 1954, the Forest View lunch room behind the car was reduced to the foundation, and in 1978 weeds grow in the cabstand to the left of the car. It seems that the only thing that never changes is change itself. — *George Krambles*

Although the Chicago Railways, its competitors and its successors would buy nearly 2,000 conventional-design streetcars following the delivery of the "Big Pullmans" in 1908 and 1909, these fine cars would outlast nearly all of the newer cars. Their heritage as a "north side cars" stems from their purchase by Chicago Railways Company, the north side operating company. Ultimately they operated throughout the city. In 1953, near the end of a 45 year career, CTA 382 is westbound on 63rd Street, a line built by Chicago City Railroads, the giant of the south side companies. Car 382 is operating beneath the Jackson Park rapid transit line at Ellis Avenue, just a short distance from the apartment of Frank Butts, where the first meeting in the organization of CERA occurred. On May 30, 1954, the last of the conventional cars operated in Chicago. — *William C. Janssen*

9

Though a large city, Chicago was divided into small neighborhood communities each with distinct ethnic character. 79th and Exchange is the heart of Cheltenham, a neighborhood originally settled by Swedes who were later joined by German and Irish immigrants. Blue collar workers took the streetcar to the steel mills of South Chicago, while professional and office workers rode the Illinois Central's Pullman-green electric commuter trains to the Loop. CTA 3278, one of CSL's multiple-unit cars built in 1924 and 1925, is making a safety stop at the I.C. Originally equipped with Tomlinson couplers, they were operated singly or in two-car trains. By this time in 1951, the Windsor Park line which turned onto Exchange had been converted to bus. Buses replaced 79th Street cars in September, much to the chagrin of those who loved the cars. — *William C. Janssen*

On October 1, 1947, CTA acquired the surface lines and rapid transit systems. The two operating divisions are represented in this September 26, 1953 view. Moving overhead are 6165 and 6166, crisply painted in mercury green and croydon cream, accented by a swamp holly orange beltrail. Surface division car 1758 swings off Lake Street southbound onto Dearborn for the one block trip to Randolph Street, where it will head back west again. In two months, Lake Street cars would cease operation east of Clinton Street, and the entire route would soon be converted to bus operation. When the 1721-1785 series cars were built in 1923 by CSL, they had Van Dorn couplers. These cars, as well as the "Old Pullmans" pulled trailers until 1930. The cars survived to be among the last conventional one-man cars operating in Chicago. —*William C. Janssen*

Exactly one year to the day after CTA began operations of the former Chicago Surface Lines system, car 5451 rests at 87th and Racine on October 1, 1948. The car is already past 40 years of service, yet it still shows its graceful lines which made this series the favorite of many fans. There were 400 of the "Big Brills." The first 100 cars, 5201 - 5300 were built in 1906. The original 50 cars were diverted to the United Railroads in San Francisco following the major earthquake and fire of that year. A second lot of cars was built by Brill for CCRy. The remaining 300 cars, 5301 - 5600, were delivered to Chicago City Railways in 1907 and 1908 as the first PAYE cars in Chicago. These cars were a continuation of a design that first appeared in 1904 on cars 5001 - 5200, which were known as the "Little Brills." — *George Krambles*

Cummings-built "Sedans" 6318 and 3371 pass on Sunday, June 24, 1951, while crossing the intersection of Indiana, Cermak and Cottage Grove on the #4/Cottage Grove Line. One hundred of the Peter Witt design cars were built in nearly equal lots by CSL's own shops, Brill and Cummings in 1929. These cars were the first in Chicago to be equipped with automatic acceleration and the first front entrance, center exit cars. Chicago Rail-ways purchased cars 3322-3381 while Chicago City Railways purchased cars 6280-6319. This was the result of CSL being a management and operating company. The first "Sedans" were received on October 3, 1929, and by Christmas the entire group was in service on the Clark-Wentworth route. They later served on Madison Street (along with PCC's) and finally on Cottage Grove. — *George Krambles*

Despite being in bankruptcy, CSL took a step toward modernization when in February 1936, they ordered 83 PCC cars from St. Louis Car Co. Nicknamed the "Blue Geese," these care were 5″ wider and 4′5″ longer than PCC's then being built for Brooklyn and Baltimore. In their original Buckingham Grey livery, modified with tiger stripes and roof details, two of these cars pass in the then sparsely settled area near the Narragansett terminal of the 63rd Street line. Assigned to the Madison Street line for almost ten years, deliveries of postwar PCC's plus contraction of route mileage allowed CTA to reassign cars such as 7017 and 4013 to 63rd Street and subsequently to Cottage Grove, Western and other lines. Unlike the post-war PCC's, these cars were scrapped without continued use of their components in rapid transit service. — *Truman Hefner*

The Roosevelt Road extension east into Grant Park was built in 1933 to serve the Century of Progress exposition. Originally, a subway terminal was planned between the Field Museum and Soldier Field. Instead, this loop was built to compete with Chicago Motor Coach buses serving the museums and nearby recreational facilities. This competition resulted as CMC operated on Chicago's boulevards, which were controlled by 22 independent Park boards, whereas CSL derived its operating rights from the City. After October 1, 1952, all routes operating into Grant Park came under the jurisdiction of CTA following the acquisition of CMC. Both CTA surface divisions are shown in this view from the pedestrian overpass. Surface Division PCC 7116 is looping while Boulevard Division ex-CMC buses swing onto eastbound 14th Boulevard. — *Truman Hefner*

Chicago's rapid transit system still serves admirably the central business district called the "Loop". Contrary to popular belief, the "Loop" does not derive its name from the elevated, but rather from the three downtown cable car loops. The rapid transit companies later formed their own loop around the district. What followed was a flurry of trains only seconds apart. Some of the trains which still circle the Loop originate at Linden Avenue in the suburb of Wilmette. In 1948, North Shore Line trains entered their own trackage after crossing Linden Avenue just out of this view to the right. The recently arrived articulated 5000's were providing midday shuttle service while the wood cars served in both peak and off-peak service. Twenty years later, except for the cars, the terminal of the Evanston line remains much the same. — *George Krambles*

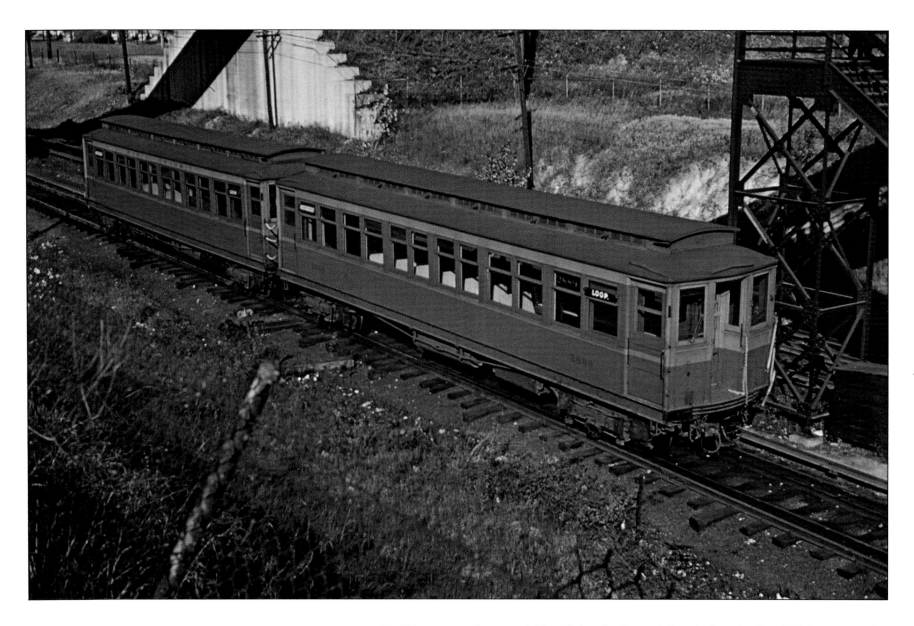

Most unusual was the Westchester line. It was constructed by the Chicago, Westchester and Western Railway, a Chicago, Aurora & Elgin subsidiary. However, train operations were conducted by the Chicago Rapid Transit Company. CRT's service to Roosevelt Road, where car 2889 is arriving in 1948, began on October 1, 1926. The trains from Chicago terminated here and a one- or two-car shuttle train carried passengers on to 22nd Street and Mannheim (LaGrange) Road after the line had been extended to there in 1930. The line's near-term objective was an Insull family real estate development named Utopia, which was to be located where Oak Brook is today. Long-term plans were a CA&E by-pass route to the Aurora branch. Neither materialized and rail service ended on December 9, 1951. — *George Krambles*

We leave Chicago on the first interurban to provide one-seat service to the Loop. Aurora, Elgin and Chicago trains began arriving at Wells Street Terminal in March, 1905. On a bitter December 18, 1951, a 1902 Stephenson motor leads a train out of the terminal, across the Chicago River and over the south trainshed of Union Station. In 1902 the car designers gave more attention to performance than crew comforts. There were no de-frosters and you couldn't stop the wind from slicing through cracks in the doors and windows of the cab. However, the bodies were originally mounted on Peckham MCB trucks and two cars were geared to achieve speeds "as much in excess of 100 miles per hour as possible." Despite high hopes, these trucks were soon replaced. However, AE&C was undoubtedly giving the fastest service of the day. — *George Krambles*

Just a little further west, CA&E and CRT's Garfield Park trains operated straight through Marshfield Junction, the major junction of the Metropolitan Elevated, where Douglas Park trains turned south and Logan Square and Humboldt Park trains turned north. All three lines passed through the roof of the Dreamland Ballroom, which was owned by the Rapid Transit Company. Imagine dancing to the rumble of your favorite traction line. In August, 1952, car 321 is on the rear of a six-car train grinding to a halt at CA&E's own Marshfield platform, which was west of the rapid transit platforms and the junction itself. CA&E service to the Loop stopped on September 20, 1953. Connecting CTA service to DesPlaines Avenue was a slow ride over temporary street level trackage along Van Buren Street. — *George Krambles*

19

CA&E's lowest numbered passenger car had a most interesting history. Built as a coach by Niles in 1902, the car was rebuilt with a baggage compartment in 1910 that was later removed and reinstalled in 1933 for funeral service. The original funeral car, 109, was equipped to train with Metropolitan Elevated cars reflecting the source of this traffic to the suburban cemeteries. It is believed that the CA&E was the last U.S. interurban to handle funerals on a regular basis. The mainline passed through or near a number of cemeteries, and the freight branch in Hillside was known variously as the Cook County or Mt. Carmel Branch, for the large cemetery in which the line once ended. In October, 1941, car 10 is spotted at the south end of Wheaton Shops. On September 10, 1948, the car was severely damaged in a collision on the "L". — *Charles A. Brown*

There was considerable sharing of equipment between the CA&E and the North Shore Line, both Insull properties. Cars of each line served the other on temporary leases. However, to meet increased suburban local traffic, twelve North Shore woods were leased in 1936 and purchased in 1946. Some of them lasted in operation until 1953. Though the CA&E raised the coupler heights, installed electric heat and modified control and jumper receptacles, it was not too practical to mix these 50 mph cars with the 60 mph CA&E cars. Thus, they were usually segregated. On August 30, 1942, though technically still owned by the North Shore, car 137 and 132 have been repainted into the CA&E livery. The cars are parked on the Batavia Station siding. The occasion was an early CERA fantrip which featured a variety of CA&E equipment. — *Charles A. Brown*

21

CA&E's penultimate car order was fifteen cars delivered by Cincinnati Car Company in 1927. Somewhat heavier than the Pullmans, they were equipped with motor-generators and battery lighting that eliminated lighting interruptions at third rail gaps. One of this group, Car 425, meets an eastbound Aurora Branch train at Diehl Road, the east end of "Batavia Junction" siding. These cars ultimately served the postwar suburban boom. However, despite its suburban traffic, the railroad maintained its interurban heritage. The 3:00 p.m. train from DesPlaines Avenue carried newspapers that filled the front vestibule and spilled into the passenger compartment, which were distributed by the motorman. Beyond Wheaton, the train slowed as the motorman flung bundles of 4 or 5 papers at road crossings—just like the delivery boy on his bicycle. — *Charles A. Brown*

Many interurbans had corporate titles which named far-off places that were never reached. The Aurora, Elgin & Chicago was an exception. Though principally a suburban carrier, beyond Wheaton it was truly an interurban. The approaches to the western terminals were picturesque runs along the Fox River. In late 1955, a "Cincy" is leaving Elgin. The setting was the same in Aurora and Batavia. Only the Geneva-St. Charles service crossed the river—twice, in fact. It crossed the river in Geneva on the Roosevelt Avenue bridge and came back across on North Avenue, St. Charles to a "terminal" on the eastern shore. Between these points the cars operated on the rails of the Aurora, Elgin and Fox River Electric, which at one time was part of the AE&C. A portion of the AE&FR remains as the Fox Valley Trolley Museum. — *Robert V. Mehlenbeck*

Wheaton was the operation's center, and where Fox Valley trains were split. Typically the first car went to Aurora, the second car to Elgin, and additional cars, if any went to the yard. The procedure was reversed for eastbound trains. On July 5, 1951, car 459 is off to Aurora. Upon their arrival in 1946, they served to keep pace with increased rush hour traffic, which required over 100 of the available 114 cars. These St. Louis-built cars were but a brief bright spot in the decline. The line's fate was debated by political bodies and in the courts. Just before noon on July 3, 1957, a court injunction expired. Orders were issued to immediately return all trains to Wheaton. While hope for revival ebbed and flowed, freight service continued until June 9, 1959. Today, some 450-series cars operate at Trolleyville, U.S.A. — *William D. Middleton*

A high speed interurban, a suburban trolley and a city streetcar—it was all of these and more—the North Shore was an institution to Chicagoans and every sailor assigned to Great Lakes. In the twilight of its existence, car 713 is leading a Shore Line special at Forest Avenue, Wilmette on May 23, 1954. The Shore Line, which opened in the summer of 1899, was in reality a suburban trolley. There was significant short-haul riding between closely spaced stations and school trippers to the end. Thursday was an unusual day requiring special service. It was "maid's day" and the live-in maids traveled from the suburbs on their day off. Domestics also provided substantial reverse direction riding during the balance of the week. Passenger service over this route, the original Evanston to Milwaukee mainline, was abandoned on July 25, 1955. — *William C. Janssen*

On September 7, 1941, car 729, sporting a homemade three-tone whistle, is southbound on a midday Sunday trip to Chicago at Highwood. This location was also known as "Highwood Pit" in deference to the inspection pits right under the mainline in front of the office building. Even on a Sunday in that bygone era, from 8:00 a.m. until 11:30 p.m. southbound Shore Line trains stopped on headways that were, at most, thirty minutes apart. Facilities were first established at Highwood in 1898. More buildings followed with the office building being constructed in 1905. Following abandonment of passenger service on the Shore Line, a remnant remained as access to the shops. The remainder of the North Shore was abandoned on January 21, 1963, after a bitter struggle to save the line. In 1978, a Ramada Inn is located on this site. — *Charles A. Brown*

Originally the North Shore Line was a local streetcar operation in Waukegan. Until the franchise expired in 1947, the North Shore Line operated a streetcar through Waukegan and down the Shore Line to Downey's (Great Lakes east entrance). At one time there were two rail routes through Waukegan. Milwaukee Express service operated via Edison Court while it was also possible to travel through downtown Waukegan and northward onto the mainline at Glen Flora Avenue. Car 359 spent most of its time in Waukegan; it finished its service in Milwaukee as shown here at Harrison Street on August 15, 1948. As in Waukegan, streetcars operated over the interurban lines—in this case to Oklahoma Avenue on Milwaukee's far south side. City rail operation continued on the NSL until August 21, 1951. — *George Krambles*

TM! Long before transcendental meditation became the rage, TM stood for one thing—The Milwaukee Electric Railway & Light Co., a utility network centered in Milwaukee and completely surrounded by the competing Insull empire. Street railway operations within the city and interurban service south to Racine, southwest to Burlington and East Troy, and west to Watertown were conducted by TM. Originally Watertown was planned to be a junction point with lines going further to Madison (west) and Jefferson (south). Instead, Watertown became a terminal when construction stopped there in 1908 due to the cost of constructing cuts up to twenty-five feet deep and fills up to thirty feet high through the area surrounding Oconomowoc. On January 28, 1940, the last day of service beyond Oconomowoc, car 1112 is pictured at Pipersville Road. — *Frank E. Butts*

The Milwaukee Northern Railway, an independent line, began service between Milwaukee and Port Washington in 1907 and reached Sheboygan in 1908. It soon became the link between two Insull properties, the North Shore Line in Milwaukee and Wisconsin Power and Light's railway in Sheboygan. Undaunted, TM's owners proposed a line to connect their traction properties in Milwaukee and Appleton. Such a line would have provided direct competition with "The Northern" as far as Cedarburg. However TM acquired "The Northern" in 1922 and nothing further came of the proposed line to Appleton. Approximately twenty years later car 1142 is stopping at Grafton. Service to Grafton and Port Washington continued under the subsequent ownership of Kenosha Motor Coach Lines from 1945 until March 28, 1948. — *Frank E. Butts*

Just prior to the abandonment of service to Sheboygan on September 23, 1940, this articulated is heading south on South 8th Street in Sheboygan. The terminal is just beyond the top of the hill in the background. Run number 3 has just crossed the Sheboygan River and a branch of the C&NW. These articulated units had an interesting history. In 1923, Cincinnati Car Co. delivered 12 combines to the Indianapolis and Cincinnati Traction Co. The cars were wholly unsuitable for the light loads on the I & C line and were replaced by Cincinnati curved-side cars in 1929. In that year eight of these cars were purchased by TM. The craftsmen at Cold Springs Shops cut the cars in two just ahead of the rear truck, and inserted a 30-foot section including an articulated joint which resulted in these two-car units. — *Frank E. Butts*

Cold Springs Shops' first attempt at an articulated unit was 1198-99. The unit was conceived as a result of a desire to provide dining service. Prevailing opinion at TM was that a standard 54-foot coach was not adequate. Articulation with vestibule connections for passenger safety was a solution to provide balance between coach, dining and kitchen space. Diner-coach service began on March 18, 1928, though practically all of TM's runs were not long enough to support dining service. After a long storage period the cars were rebuilt as straight coaches in 1942. On April 4, 1943, the unit is inbound from Waukesha. It is on 6th Street approaching Michigan alongside the North Shore Line station. These cars were extensively used on the Port Washington line. However, the single entrance door made them early retirement candidates. — *Charles A. Brown*

Between 1925 and 1930 TM built a new line on private right-of-way from 8th Street to West Junction. Previously, the interurbans operated over city streets to reach downtown. To end the hazards of mixed operation of heavy interurbans and lighter streetcars, (which ironically hastened the demise of TM's successor) three former Milwaukee Northern wood cars were rebuilt in 1930 to a double-end configuration, with air operated doors and MU control but incredibly no couplers. These cars replaced two 600-series streetcars in local service over the new Rapid Transit Line to West Junction. The graceful lines of the arch windows, a trademark of these Niles-built cars, were covered over in the rebuilding. On May 12, 1942, car 1102, the first of the group, is heading west on Clybourn to enter the Rapid Transit Line just short of 8th Street. — *Charles A. Brown*

Turning toward the east on our journey into yesterday we stop in Gary. From 1908 to 1947 Gary had a truly fascinating system. Like TM it had city streetcars, suburban trolleys (Hammond, Hobart and Crown Point) and an interurban line (Valparaiso). On May 2, 1942, car 12 is approaching the Nickel Plate Railroad crossing as it is returning from Hammond to Gary. The route to Hammond was not particularly scenic as it traversed a heavily industralized area. However, the line to Valpariso was different. "Valpo" was very much out in the country, particularly south of Woodville. From there the line skirted three lakes and crossed rolling terrain as it approached "Valpo." It was the destination of many trolley trips from the city until the line was abandoned on October 22, 1938. The final streetcar in Gary operated on February 28, 1947. — *Charles A. Brown*

Samuel Insull's greatest railroad venture was the South Shore. As Sam Jr. said, the Lake Shore was nothing but "a broken down pile of junk." But it had one redeeming quality—freight service. The Lake Shore could haul coal to the generating plants in Michigan City. This fit in well with Insull's obsession to participate in the movement of coal to his utilities. Thus Insull acquired the bonds (construction loans) and 60% of stock from Cleveland Trust to gain control of the railroad. In August 1953 Motor 1008 is on Chicago Avenue at Indianapolis Blvd. The East Chicago station was just beyond the Vogel Theatre. Finally in 1956 the trains left the street to use a by-pass route acquired in 1926. The thirty year delay started, according to Sam Jr., because the Insull family was not about to pay "a ransom to some tin horn mayor". — *William C. Janssen*

Passenger service on the Lake Shore was provided by these massive Niles motor cars. Their tremendous power was illustrated in 1926 when one motor pulled six heavyweight Illinois Central coaches. Really, they were locomotives and the Lake Shore used them as such. Originally a 6,600-volt single phase A.C. system, the line was converted to 1,500-volt D.C. to provide for operation over the IC to Chicago's Loop. On August 29, 1926, the South Shore finally offered full, direct service downtown. It was the last of the "Big Three" Chicago interurbans to do so. Line car 1101 was one of a handful of Lake Shore cars to survive. The re-electrification of this car was a project of Charles E. Keevil, one of the many Chicago Rapid Transit people temporarily assigned to Michigan City to assist in the rehabilitation. — *Charles A. Brown*

Service on the Lake Shore was a haphazard affair. By contrast, the South Shore provided 56 daily trains; however, were it not for the tenacity of Charlie Jones and other members of management this passenger service would have fallen victim to the Depression. From this famine, World War II brought short-lived prosperity. In August 1942, car 5 is leaving the east end of Davis siding. Signals at Davis, just east of Michigan City, were controlled by the dispatcher. Westward trains, though superior, could be held for late eastward trains. Based on a review of operating timetable #96, then in effect, we suspect this to be the case, as no meets were scheduled at Davis. The board to control these signals is still existent, at Shops. It is a living tribute to Insull, Jones and many others that the trains still run in 1978. — *Charles A. Brown*

Street railway service in South Bend was provided by the Chicago South Bend and Northern Indiana Railway. This service was provided by an incredible assortment of cars from the company's predecessors as well as the two sources portrayed here. Both of these cars were built as trailers and later motorized. Car 173 was built by Brill for the Cleveland Railway. Car 216, the second car on the NI assigned that number, was built by St. Louis Car for the St. Joseph Valley Railway. They were acquired by the NI in 1923 and 1921 repectively, and ran until city service ended on June 15, 1940. On June 25, 1939, these two cars were on a CERA fan trip at Notre Dame University. The fans came to South Bend on a special six-car South Shore train that included a parlor car and car 35 equipped as a lunch counter car specifically for the excursion. — *Frank E. Butts*

Local interests owned the Lafayette Street Railway during two periods of its history. Originally incorporated in 1883 the company was acquired by the Fort Wayne and Wabash Valley Traction Co., a predecessor of Indiana Service Corporation. Reorganization followed bankruptcy and local interests were back in control, operating under the original name. Local ownership was widely hailed as one reason for its success. Institution of one man service with 18 Birneys, like 26 and 24 passing at 24th and Kossuth on February 17, 1940, was credited for a 27% reduction in labor costs. Despite disposal of the power plant and elimination of assessments the 32,000 citizens of Lafayette and West Lafayette saw their city cars, as well as the Purdue University test car, operate for the last time on May 11, 1940. — *Frank E. Butts*

Resplendent in its post war livery, the first of Indianapolis Railways' ninety Brill lightweights begins a trip at 42nd and Crown Hill to downtown. Street railway service began in Indianapolis on Illinois Street in 1864 and was extended, in 1867 to Crown Hill cemetery, where this car is shown. Indianapolis Railways was controlled by the Terre Haute Indianapolis & Eastern Traction which in part explains why the street railway company built the famed Traction Terminal. After many years of falling behind in equipment modernization the company took a giant stride in the midst of the Depression. These cars arrived from Brill in 1933. They were the only cars operating at the end of streetcar service. The Illinois line was converted in October, 1951. The end of street railway service in Indiana came on January 11, 1953. — *Robert V. Mehlenbeck*

Union Traction Company of Indiana was one of the pioneer electric railway lines in the midwest. Its founder was Charles L. Henry who is credited with the coining the word "interurban". On July 2, 1930, Union Traction was purchased by an Insull holding company. Their primary interest was the power generating territory rights to link-up other rural electrification networks. Railway operations were spun off into the Indiana Railroad. High speed luxury cars were seen as a salvation. Car 58, one of fourteen coach-lounge cars built by American Car & Foundry in 1931, pauses at Springport, a stop on the New Castle-Muncie route. Howard Odinius and John Humiston look on as L. M. Brown, General Superintendent of the IR pauses for refreshment at the spring that gave the town its name. — *James P. Shuman*

Car 58 was operating on CERA fantrip number 3. This trip was held on August 20, 1938 and was attended by 15 people who traveled on a "Fort Wayne loop" from Indianapolis. Here the car is entering New Castle en route from Muncie. What had begun as a nearly 700-mile empire with almost 300 scheduled trips daily ended just 11 years later as a single 62-mile run. Looking back, Sam Insull, Jr., the president of IR says that thinking he could save the Indiana Railroad was his biggest mistake in business. "We totally underestimated the impact of the automobile". With the demise of the system the 35 lightweights entered forced retirement, most with less than 10 years of service. The finest modern interurban cars were available at $1,000 each. There were virtually no takers. Only two cars were purchased! — *Frank E. Butts*

By October 20, 1942, when RPO 376 ventured out on CERA fan trip 27 the system was down to two lines. Ft. Wayne-New Castle-Indianapolis service stopped on January 19, 1941. All services ended on September 8, 1941 when the lone franchise car to Seymour met the line car head-on on a blind curve south of Columbus. The Indiana Railroad and its predecessors were an amalgam of companies. Car 376 was purchased by the Indiana Service Corporation in 1926. This classic photograph is on the White River Bridge between Anderson and Muncie. It truly reflects the Indiana Railroad. An Indiana Service Corporation car on a bridge that was built by the Union Traction Company of Indiana. We would be remiss if we didn't note one more time that 376 is the last IR car in service. It is line car 1100 on the South Shore Line. — *Frank E. Butts*

Rolling west across Possum Trot trestle, Illinois Terminal car 263 has just left Danville, on October 13, 1951, for a 120-mile run to Springfield. Wooden trestles, while impressive photographic subjects, are maintenance headaches. Those on principal routes are replaced, while on lesser routes they survive. This trestle was a harbinger of the line's early demise, it survived until the end. The original interurban service on "The Traction" began in 1903, between Danville and Champaign. Almost fifty years later, service into Danville succumbed to highway construction. Thus Danville, the first city to be served, was the first city to lose service when the line was cut back on April 27, 1952, to a grain elevator at Watkins. This incredible operation, ended when passenger service was further cut back to Champaign on April 26, 1953. — *Gordon E. Lloyd*

Construction of the remaining I.T. lines began westward from Decatur in 1903. The final segment, Lincoln to Mackinaw Junction was completed in 1908. This segment was within the 3,300-volt AC operation that extended from Bloomington and Springfield to Peoria. Conversion to the standard 600-volt DC potential came in 1909. But, whatever the voltage, excellent passenger service was I.T.'s trademark. On the beautiful autumn morning of October 13, 1941, car 277, a 1913 product of St. Louis Car Co., is leaving Peoria to tackle one of the most demanding limited train schedules. Train 91 covered the 174 miles to St. Louis, at an average speed of 43.5 mph, in four hours; 25 minutes faster than the ''Illmo Limited'' and over an hour quicker than local train 89. In 1978, car 277 can be ridden at the Illinois Railway Museum. — *Charles A. Brown*

Peoria Railway was the largest of Illinois Traction's street railway operations and its successors lasted the longest. On Saturday, October 12, 1940, Illinois Power Co. 471 is at Bradley and Rebecca. The Bradley line was named for the street and University it served. Main Street cars used this trackage in the opposite direction. Service on this line was interrupted circa 1921, when the poles supporting the trolley wires around the corner of Bradley and Western fell, bringing the overhead down into the street. On June 30, 1928, trackage on Bradley was abandoned. Yielding to complaints, service was restored on February 1, 1930. As only the trolley wire was removed, restoration of service was relatively easy. The last streetcar in Peoria pulled in at 12:45 a.m. on October 3, 1946 and the last I.T. interurban left East Peoria on June 12, 1955. — *Robert V. Mehlenbeck*

Significant freight car loadings and joint tariffs with steam roads as early as 1910 set the I.T. apart from most interurbans and accounts for the road's survival. Virtually all of its freight motors were home built of distinctive design. The Class B and C locomotives reflected the architectural concepts of Master Mechanic J. M. Bosenbury. Starting in 1940, five Class C locomotives were converted to Class D. Motor 72, nee class C 1591, was 55'5" long and weighed 217,000 pounds. The locomotive seems about as massive as anything to operate on the streets of Morton—yet just eight years later the I.T. purchased ALCO-GE diesel road switchers that were nearly ten tons heavier. GP-7's followed and by May of 1969 there were SD-39's nearly twice as heavy as the class D's. Consider that weight on track constructed for interurbans. — *George Krambles*

I.T. had a fine tradition of first class deluxe service utilizing a fleet of six parlor-buffet-observation cars. Faced with a well maintained but aging fleet of electric cars and the onslaught of high-speed and in some cases, streamlined steamroad trains, the I.T. responded in the best way it could. A. P. Titus, the president of the line, captured, in 1941, the spirit of this drive. In a hand written note to employees in operating timetable 13 he advised, "our success . . . depends largely on the service we render the public. We are improving our equipment, track and roadway spending more than what sometimes seems justified." One result was the air-conditioned, reserved seat "Illmo Limited" at Lincoln, on October 5, 1941. These refurbished standard cars remained in daily service until the arrival of the streamliners in 1948 and 1949. — *Charles A. Brown*

All of this spending was going on while the Indiana Railroad lightweights were available at $1,000 each. A few years later the I.T. spent enough money on eight streamlined cars to have purchased 1,000 of the used high-speeds. As the inauguration of streamlined service neared, a few of the standard cars received modernized interiors and this curious "whisker" treatment. Car 285 is at Granite City Belt Line Junction. The second car, with its single vestibule, is worth noting. It is either the former "Missouri" or "Illinois". They were rebuilt as "room sleepers" in 1930 from a parlor observation car and a straight coach. Instead of berths, there were nine rooms with regular beds. These cars were rebuilt, again, as coaches in 1941, following the termination of sleeper service between St. Louis and Peoria on August 31, 1940. — *Charles A. Brown*

The last expansions of the system came in 1928 when the Illinois Terminal Railroad, a steam line that ran between Alton and Edwardsville, and in 1930 when the St. Louis and Alton Railway were acquired. Car 101 was built for the Alton Granite and St. Louis Traction Co. That line was leased to the East St. Louis and Suburban in 1906. It was the Illinois Traction's route into St. Louis between 1905 and 1910. I.T. acquired the A. G. & St. L. from the E. St. L. & S. By then the A. G. & St. L. was known as the St. Louis and Alton. Despite the corporate complex, car 101, seen in Granite City, served its various owners until service to Alton ended on March 7, 1953. I.T.'s last passenger service was the local streetcar to Granite City. It stopped running on June 22, 1958, the same day that streetcar service ended in Chicago. — *Robert V. Mehlenbeck*

On September 3, 1954 "the Traction" was in its twilight. Despite the late date, a ritual that at one time was repeated daily throughout the country was still being practiced in Monticello. Express is being transferred from the car to a Railway Express truck. From the beginning express and less-than-carload traffic was a significant part of I.T.'s operations. By 1910 carload freight operations were already greater than its L.C.L. business.

All was not this tranquil in 1919. I.T. formed its own express operation as a result of a dispute with REA predecessor American Railway Express. Maybe this was foresight as REA is out of business but the I.T. is still hauling freight. Just east of Monticello track is being relaid on the former I.T. right-of-way by the Monticello & Sangamon Valley, a steam railway museum operation. — *Gordon E. Lloyd*

Ohio was the pinnacle of interurban operation. Unfortunately, it was all virtually gone by the time color film was commercially available. However, a few street railways still operated. We enter the state over its namesake river on the "Green Line", officially the Cincinnati, Newport & Covington Railway. The cars began their northeasterly journey at Fort Mitchell, Kentucky, and ran over private right-of-way to Devou Park where southbound car 517 is stopping. From there the cars operated on Dixie Highway to the shore of the Ohio River. There they raised the second trolley pole on the car to travel on the Cincinnati Street Railway to Dixie Terminal. The Ohio River crossing was on John Roebling's classic suspension bridge that opened in 1866. Roebling also designed the Brooklyn Bridge. — *Frank E. Butts*

Cincinnati's street railway was distinctive with its second trolley wire. Following a dispute with the phone company the second wire was installed to prevent stray return current from allegedly causing interference with the phone circuits. The last of the standard heavyweight streetcars for the Cincinnati Traction Company were series 2200-2304 built by Cincinnati Car Co. in 1919. In 1920 the car company suffered a lengthy strike. The Traction Company's next purchase would be the "curved-sides" of 1923. The 2200's were notable for use of a two motor Eliot 50 D truck. Unit cost of the 105 cars was $7,000. They served Cincinnati for 30 years. Car 2258, the last of the series to operate, is at Delta and Eastern Avenues, the terminal of the 68/Madison-Delta line. The last streetcar ran in the "Queen City" in 1951. — *George Krambles*

Kentucky-born Tom Johnson purchased Cleveland's Brooklyn Street Railway in 1879. Johnson's battles with Mark Hanna over traction issues and Johnson's advocacy of municipal ownership were legendary. Resolution of these matters came in 1910, when the receivers were discharged and a new franchise established a partnership between the city and a new company, Cleveland Railways. Cleveland's last acquisition was 25 PCC cars, 4250-4274, which like Johnson came by way of Kentucky. Built by St. Louis Car Co. for Louisville, only ten cars were delivered there before the order was cancelled. After being sold to Cleveland they served for only six years. On September 9, 1951, car 4251 is at the Public Square in downtown Cleveland. In 1952, together with Cleveland's original fifty Pullman-built PCC's, this series was sold to Toronto. — *George Krambles*

In 1923 the Monongahela West Penn Public Service Company resulted from the merger of a series of underlying companies. Among them was the Fairmont and Clarksburg Traction Co. which became the main division of the MWP. During World War II this line provided yeoman service by carrying crowds of passengers and much carload freight. Just a little southwest of Fairmont, West Virginia was Edgemont Junction. On Oc-tober 26, 1941, Jewett-built 286 is on the interurban run through the West Fork River valley to Clarksburg. With the interurban on its way the two city cars will continue to their loops in Fairmont. Car 331 will retrace the interurban's route down Fleming and Fairmont Avenues while the other Cincinnati Curveside, car 328 will head out Locust Avenue. Both cars will meet again in downtown Fairmont. — *James P. Shuman*

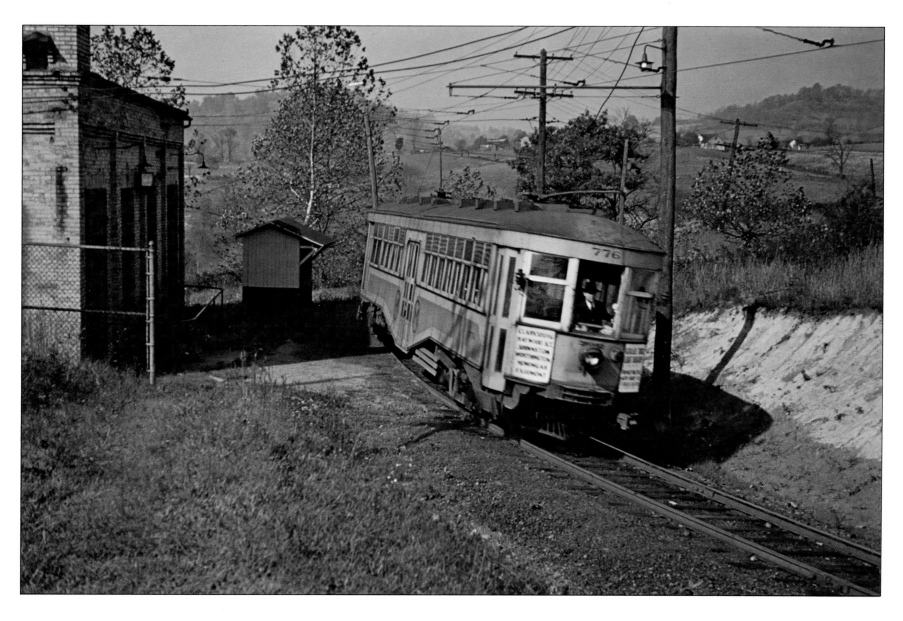

In an era when Interstate 79 allows one to drive the 20-plus miles between Fairmont and Clarksburg on an almost straight route it hardly seems probable that the MWP (and B&O) would select so tortuous a route as the railroads followed. What seems even more improbable is that MWP provided frequent service including, for a short period of time beginning in 1926, deluxe parlor car service with car 776. Perhaps more than any other thing, car 776, and its sister 775, represented the influence of MWP's owner, the West Penn System. In its glory days, car 776, named *West Virginia* instead of carrying its car number, made four daily round trips in the limited-stop extra fare parlor car service. By October, 1941 the car, shorn of its parlor section and its name, maintains a local schedule en route to Fairmont. All service ended in 1947. — *James P. Shuman*

Street Railway service in Pittsburgh began in 1859 and in 1901 Pittsburgh Railways was formed as a consolidation of many smaller companies. The system ultimately grew in size to become second in size only to Chicago. Though similar in appearance to many city cars, 3752 was one of twenty cars built by Standard Car Company in 1925 with multiple-unit control, high back plush seats and a smoking compartment for interurban service on the Charleroi Line. At the time of this trip from West Library, near the present terminus of the line, the cars resembled standard city cars. This low-floor "Pittsburgh Standard" car is inbound at St. Anne's stop, the city fare zone limit, which is located about halfway between Castle Shannon and Washington Junction. Over 850 of these cars were built between 1915 and 1927; some survived until 1956. — *Charles A. Brown*

What became the Charleroi line had its beginnings in 1889 as the Monongahela Street Railway. Service to Pittsburgh began in 1904 over Route 42-Dormont. In 1909, electrified service began over the present route through Saw Mill Run Valley. Service was provided by classic Kuhlman wooden combination cars followed by low-floor and Peter Witt cars. Pittsburgh's last conventional cars were 15 interurbans delivered by St. Louis Car Co. in 1928. One of these 3800-series cars is at Allenport having just crossed under the Pittsburgh and West Virginia Railroad (now Norfolk and Western) on its northbound trip from Roscoe to Charleroi and Pittsburgh. These cars were phased out of service by the end of 1950. Operations beyond Simmons (now Library Loop) were abandoned in the morning of Sunday, June 28, 1953. — *Charles A. Brown*

Primarily used for carrying sand, workcar M130, formerly car 3396, is at Tylerdale Carbarn in Washington, Pennsylvania on June 11, 1950. Within three years, Pittsburgh Railways Co.'s service to and in Washington would end. The last run beyond Drake was during the night of August 29, 1953, closing out 50 years of service. In 1903 the Washington and Cannonsburg Railway began operations between these two cities. Six years later, the line was opened from Canonsburg to Washington Jct. This was truly a high-speed interurban line with over 25 bridges spanning highways, railroads and watercourses. These bridges ranged up to 1,055 feet long and one was 80 feet high. Considerable grading and filling completed the line's profile. Today little remains except for the Pennsylvania Railway Museum at Arden, just a few miles north of Washington. — *Frank B. Fairbanks*

South Hills Junction continues to be the focal point of street railway operations, with South Hills (formerly Tunnel) car house nestled in the valley behind the junction. As late as 1966, nine carlines converged at this point before proceeding to downtown Pittsburgh. PCC 1458 was operating on Route 44-Knoxville on March 21, 1953. Service on this route terminated on November 14, 1971, the same day that service ended on the two other "Hilltop" lines—49-Beltzhoover and 53-Carrick. Route 35-Library, 36-Drake, 38-Mt. Lebanon and 42-Dormont cars stll use the tracks in the foreground while route 49-Arlington/Warrington cars use the tracks adjacent to 1458. Since 1976, buses have shared the Mt. Washington tunnel with streetcars as a part of the South PATway busway. — *Frank B. Fairbanks*

Bright orange center door cars, like 732 and 736, meeting at Armbrust siding near Hecla Junction, were the trademark of West Penn Railways. Forty almost identical cars were built, a few at a time, by both the West Penn and Cincinnati Car Co. between 1910 and 1925 for use on the lines radiating out of Connellsville and Uniontown. Riders of these cars immediately noticed the absence of a typical trolley sound—the air com-

pressor. These cars were equipped with a combination electric and hand brake system. Hand operated controllers provided dynamic braking connections between the motors and magnetic track brakes hung between the wheels. Final stopping and holding of the car was accomplished by hand brake applications. West Penn used magnetic track brakes years before they became standard on the PCC car. — *Robert V. Mehlenbeck*

West Penn's operations in the coal and coke region of southwestern Pennsylvania continued into the 1950's. Miners continued to use the interurbans to travel from work as they were reluctant to get their shiny new autos dirty. The auto finally conquered. However, the final decline in ridership was caused by Pittsburgh's TV stations finally reaching the area. Local service was provided by a variety of cars. One of them was 212, one of twenty-five built by Stephenson in 1901 with Brill 27-E-1 trucks. The 200-series were the first cars to be equipped with magnetic track brakes. Most of the cars in this series were scrapped between 1936 and 1938. But car 212, which was at Connellsville Shops on August 31, 1941, was one of two which survived until 1951. The last of the orange cars arrived in Uniontown from Connellsville on August 9, 1952. — *James P. Shuman*

Johnstown is located in the southern reaches of Cambria County. Perhaps better known for its floods and economic misfortune, Johnstown was a favorite of railfans. The accommodating management of Johnstown Traction Co. allowed many large and small fantrips. The appeal was in the variety of equipment and environment that the system offered. Conventional cars survived until the end of service due to the lack of turning facilities on some routes. In June, 1952, car 211 is en route to Southmont. Shade tree-lined streets, steep grades and single-track operation made this lightly traveled branch of the Roxbury line a pleasure to ride. However, the lack of patronage reduced service to a daily franchise run. The branch was converted to bus in October, 1954, when a rock slide blocked the track. — *William C. Janssen*

Modern PCC cars seemed incongruous amid the grime of aging basic steel manufacturing facilities in the small city of Johnstown. Seventeen all-electric cars were delivered by St. Louis Car in January and February, 1947. On May 31st, 1947, car 404 is climbing the long grade in the center reservation of Roxbury Avenue near the end of the Roxbury Line in the southeastern part of the town. Car 404's destination sign displays its point of origin, Coopersdale, and has traveled through downtown from the southwestern corner of town. Trolley service on the Roxbury line and in Johnstown ended on April 11, 1960. Shortly after 6:00 p.m. that day, four fantrip cars, two special cars for civic representatives, and the last revenue car paraded from city hall to Moxham car barn. After 69 years of electric service the power was shut off. — *James P. Shuman*

At one time there was 123 miles of street railway trackage in the Logan Valley. The huge Pennsylvania Railroad Shop complex generated sufficient local traffic but to promote more suburban passenger traffic, City Passenger Railway, the predecessor of the Altoona and Logan Valley Electric Railway, developed and opened Lakemont Park in 1894. The park proved to be a positive influence in the development of South Altoona and the surrounding area. By Memorial Day, 1947, only a few of the picnickers at Lakemont Park had arrived by trolley. An ex-Ohio Valley Electric car, one of eight built by St. Louis Car Co. in 1913, all of which served the A&VL since 1918 heads back to Altoona after completing a tripper run to the park. The line to the right continues to Hollidaysburg. Service on the final lines ended on August 7, 1954. — *James P. Shuman*

"Clinton's Big Ditch," as the Erie Canal was known, opened in 1825. After the turn of the century, a bypass around Rochester opened and the main channel through the city was abandoned in 1919. Soon thereafter plans were advanced to construct an electric railway along the canal's right-of-way. The Rochester Subway and Industrial Railroad was organized to provide both passenger and freight service. On December 1, 1927, the New York State Railways, under contract with the city, commenced operations. In the early 1950's, car 52 has completed another run on the nine mile line. This 1916 product of Cincinnati was assigned to interurban service out of Utica until 1938. Following World War II, the line was overgrown with weeds as evidenced by the clean equalizers on the trucks. The end was near, as the line closed on June 30, 1956. — *J. Schmit*

Unlike the United States, where the power companies owned the interurbans, or radial railways, as they were known in Canada, most of the lines in Ontario and Quebec were owned by the stream railroads. The Niagara, St. Catherines and Toronto Railway was a Canadian National Railways operation that crossed the 25-mile wide Niagara peninsula. The Railway never reached Toronto, but it was a line of contrasts—picturesque settings and industrial drab. On July 4, 1953, one of the classic Preston-built cars was in service near Welland. These cars would warm the heart of any traction fan as they creaked and swayed along the rough track. This line, which started in 1879 as a horsecar operation in St. Catherines, survived to become Ontario's last interurban. Passenger service was abandoned on March 28, 1959. — *William C. Janssen*

Canadian Pacific Railway's interurbans were the Grand River Railway, and Lake Erie and Northern Railway. Though separate companies, they operated as one with the pooling of all resources. The GRR began as a street railway in 1894, and its successors were leased by the CPR in 1908. CPR leased the LE&N in 1914, before the line was completed. Technically, the GRR operated between Waterloo, Ontario and Galt (since 1973 a part of Cambridge) while the LE&N continued southward from Galt to Port Dover on the northern shore of Lake Erie. CPR's influence is evident in the design and color of the substantial cars built by Preston Car and Coach between 1915 and 1921. Two of these cars are shown, circa 1950, along the Grand River. Abandonment of the combined lines' passenger service came on April 23, 1955. — *Robert V. Mehlenbeck*

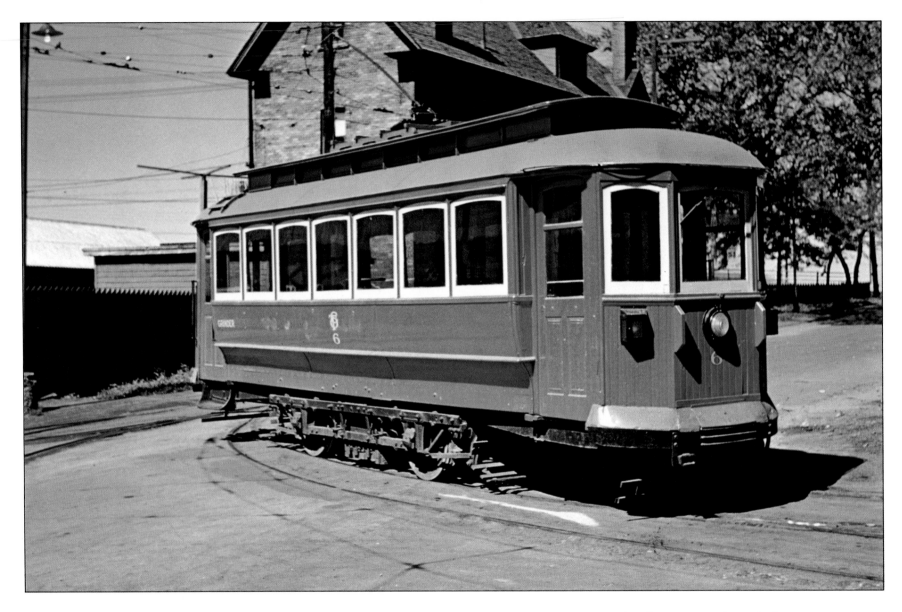

Ottawa was chosen in 1857 to be the seat of the Canadian government. Public transportation began in 1870. By 1893, an amalganation of horse and electric railways existed when the Ottawa Electric Railway was formed. One of the new company's most conspicuous products was its home-built fleet. Car 6 is a classic example. This Ottawa-built 1897 single trucker holds the honor of being the oldest piece of equipment chronicled in this book. In that era a closed car was used mostly in winter as a companion fleet of open car bodies would be stored in the carbarn awaiting summer. The car bodies were switched randomly among the supply of trucks. On September 9, 1951, this well-preserved 54-year old car was in service as a rail grinder shown here on the ladder tracks in front of Champagne car house. — *George Krambles*

To quote the company, Ottawa "was blessed with a most favourable hydraulic site" so it naturally progressed to an early electric operation. By 1905, there was 115 passenger cars. In Canada, only Toronto and Montreal had more cars. A curiosity of Ottawa Transportation Commission's roster was that only snow-sweeper 7 carried that number. Apparently that policy arose from alleged superstition of the president following an early accident of car 37. The common superstition of 13 did not prevail. On July 6, 1957, home-built car 813, a design and color scheme vaguely reminiscent of Chicago's "Pullmans", was still in service. This series together with the 900's provided the bulk of the service in the last years. When service ended on May 1, 1959, the company had built or purchased only cars of conventional design. — *Frank E. Butts*

Toronto and Detroit have stunning similarities in their transit histories. Both created municipal operations to compete with, and ultimately take over, privately owned lines. Each had a flirtation with Birneys and a man named Couzens; H. H. in Toronto and "Big Jim" in Detroit. And — the Peter Witt dominated. Before the Toronto Transportation Commission carried its first passenger it had ordered 110 trailers and 140 Peter Witts, two of which were delivered before the September 1, 1921, takeover date. Motor-trailer operation continued until the Yonge Subway opened on March 30, 1954. Five days thereafter the Upper Canada Railway Society chartered "Big Witt" 2932 and a "Q" Class trailer as TTC's last trailer train. In 1978, streetcars continue to serve Toronto and their future is bright. — *Raymond F. Corley*

Montreal Tramways Company was most active in car design but slow to adopt one-man operation. The world's first "pay-as-you-enter" (PAYE) car was constructed for Tramways in 1905. In 1907, MTC followed with world's first all-steel streetcar which was built by Pressed Steel Car Co. This trend continued with train operation and two three-truck, two-man articulated cars. The introduction of one-man cars was cautious. Fourteen Birneys were purchased used from Detroit after selective testing with existing cars. Finally, in 1926, car 1900, the first of the one-man/two-man cars was received. By 1929, the 111 one-man cars, including 2002, had been delivered. On October 31, 1951, car 2002 is traversing the well-known Mountain line on the rugged northern slope of Mount Royal as it served route 93—Remembrance Road. — *William E. Robertson*

The geographical orientation of Montreal on an island in the St. Lawrence River creates many mutations of the compass. Montreal South and the "southern counties" are really east of Montreal. However, trains of the Montreal & Southern Counties leaving the McGill Street Terminal in Montreal first went west before turning east to cross the Victoria Bridge near St. Lambert, where the general offices and car shops were located. From St. Lambert there was a branchline that went north to reach Montreal South. Service on this branch, which at one time reached Longueil, was usually maintained by a single car like 326. The 320-series had an interesting history. They were built by Brill as trailers for the Washington and Virginia Railway, who sold them to the Niagara, St. Catherines & Toronto. In 1947, they came to the M&SC. — *George Krambles*

Originally, the Central Vermont Railway dispatchers at St. Albans, Vermont, controlled the line. This international flavor was maintained to the end, as train orders were given in English and repeated in French. Unfortunately for the railroad, most of the traffic went into Montreal. The single track on Victoria Bridge became an Achilles' Heel. Only a 20-minute headway could be operated across the bridge. Despite the line's continued financial problems, one could still find vestiges of its glory days. Crisply maintained car 607 posed between runs in Montreal. This classic single-end wood car was one of twelve built between 1917 and 1923 by Ottawa Car Co. Forty-five years of service ended on October 13, 1956, when plans to reconstruct Victoria Bridge for the St. Lawrence Seaway excluded the M&SC. — *George Krambles*

A ride on the Quebec Railway Light and Power Company afforded many views of scenery and historical landmarks in the heart of French Canada. From the quaint environs of Quebec City, the line operated northeast on a double track line to Montmorency Falls, where Car 410 is turning on the wye in 1948. Beyond there, a single track was nestled between the cliffs of the Laurentians and the shore of the St. Lawrence River as it passed through the oldest villages on the Beaupre Coast. To the end of service the company operated wood cars, including the survivors of a group of thirty open platform trailers built by Jackson & Sharp in 1889. Car 410 is one of ten single end cars built by Ottawa Car Co. between 1902 and 1910. Members of the series had an unusual history of alternately being rebuilt as motors or trailers. — *George Krambles*

While an attraction, the 274-foot Montmorency Falls was not the reason for construction, in 1889, of the Quebec, Montmorency & Charlevoix Railway. Rather, it was Canada's first Catholic pilgrimage center, the Basilica of Sainte Anne de Beaupre. Proximity of power sources led the new owners QRL&P to electrify in 1900. Intended to go farther, the electrification reached only 25 miles to St. Joachim. Beyond was the discon- nected Canadian National Murray Bay Subdivision, extending 67 miles to Clermont, which explains why the CN purchased the QRL&P on November 1, 1951. Just prior to CN ownership, car 455, one of only six steel cars owned by the line, built by Ottawa Car Co. in 1930, is at the Falls on September 4, 1951. Electric operations ended on March 15, 1959; however, CN freight service continues in 1978. — *George Krambles*

York Utilities Company succeeded the Atlantic Shore Railway; however, for most of its existence it operated only two lines which totaled 4.54 miles. In March, 1942, car 80 and its sister 82 ran on the 2.44 mile line between Sanford and Springdale, Maine. Designed by Charles O. Birney, this type of car was first introduced in Everett, Washington on October 23, 1916. As quickly as Birney cars were built, a second-hand market sprang up. YU purchased eight used Birneys from three properties. Cars 80 and 82 were built in 1919, to 3'6" gauge, for the Denver & South Platte Railway. When sold to YU in 1927, the trucks were widened to standard gauge. This was the last job done in the ASL's Town House shops in Kennebunkport. These cars are preserved at Seashore Trolley Museum. — *Norton D. Clark*

Union Street Railway survived to become the last small city trolley operation in Massachusetts. Thirty years separate the building, by Osgood-Bradley Car Co., of Electromobile 601 and semi-convertible 283. They, along with 1922 lightweights and old interurbans, served the Lunds Corner—Fort Rodman "mainline" until its conversion on May 3, 1947. Known locally as the "Yellow Belly cars", the 280-series cars were principally used as rush hour trippers, these cars were a favorite of fans. On June 16, 1940, car 283 is at Fort Rodman on a charter trip. Car 601, which was delivered to USR on its own wheels via the Boston & Worchester and Eastern Massachusetts Street Railway, was one of seven cars sold to the Queensboro Bridge Railway. On April 7, 1957, it operated the last streetcar trip in New York City. — *Norton D. Clark*

To avoid the capital investment in duplicate sets of open and closed body cars, the "convertible" car was developed. Its side panels could be removed or slid into roof pockets. A more practical arrangement was the "semi-convertible" car. Various types of window sashes, which could be removed or slid or folded into the car body or roof, distinguished this type of car. Eastern Massachusetts Street Railway car 4390 is one of the 200 semi-convertibles built by Laconia Car Co. in 1917-1918 for EM's predecessor, Bay State Street Railway. On October 13, 1941, the car is ending a run at the Boston & Maine's Farm Street Station in Stoneham. This route ran from the Boston Elevated's Sullivan Square station via the Fellsway reservation (private right-of-way) to Stoneham until 1946. The line was one of the most scenic in the Boston area. — *Norton D. Clark*

In its search for a suitable lightweight car, Boston Elevated Railway's engineers considered the Birney but found it poorly adapted for their operations. So, they designed their own car. Between 1922 and 1928, 471 of the so-called Type 5 cars were built by four builders. To achieve the 31,000 pound weight and low cost, commercial steel shapes and side sheeting and spartan interior appointments were utilized. So zealous were the designers that there was not even a headliner inside the car. As a result, in later years the cars were mechanically sound but had leaky roofs and rusted side sheeting. In its last years, car 5643, a 1923 Laconia product, is leaving Mattapan on route 29 to Egleston station. The last regular service operation of these cars was in 1959. Sister car 5645 has been preserved at the Warehouse Point Trolley Museum. — *William C. Janssen*

Rapid Transit is a significant part of Boston's history. America's first subway opened under Tremont Street on September 1, 1897, for streetcars. On June 10, 1901, the ''Main Line El'' opened between Sullivan Square and Dudley. Its trains shared the Tremont subway until November 29, 1908, when the Washington Street tunnel opened. There was a period of transition when PCC 3304 passed these venerable elevated cars at North Station on June 15, 1955. PCC 3304, one of the last ordered new by Boston, was built in 1951 by Pullman, who also built new Orange Line elevated cars in 1957. On April 7, 1975, Orange Line trains started using a new subway line under the Charles River to first, Sullivan Square, and on to Oak Grove on March 12, 1977. In 1978, the PCC's still operate and new cars and line extensions are being constructed. — *William C. Janssen*

Providence is New England's second largest city but it has been without streetcar service since May 15, 1948, when final ceremonies were held, appropriately, at the Swan Point Cemetery end of the Butler line. Union Electric Railways was the last operating company. Its bright yellow cars, like 2065, shown here on Broad Street in September, 1941, at one time operated over 320 route miles. Car 2065 was one of 150 cars built by Osgood-Bradley in 1923. They were a simple but utilitarian vehicle. Some were resold to Washington, D. C. and Mexico City. UER was formed in 1921, from the remains of the Rhode Island Company. RICo. was one of the largest traction systems in the country, offering freight and passenger service throughout the state and connected with the giant Bay State Street Railway of Massachusetts. — *Norton D. Clark*

The Connecticut Company was formed in 1907 and grew through lease arrangements to become the second-largest trolley network in New England. Only the Bay State Railway was larger. The greatest growth came on February 28, 1910, when the New Haven Railroad leased all of its electric street railways in Connecticut to the company. The Depression hit the area hard, and bus conversions followed bankruptcy of the underlying companies. Best known to many people were the 85 open cars that carried incredible loads to the Yale Bowl until November 22, 1947. While it is interesting to speculate on the number of people who could crowd onto a car, one often wonders how many fares were collected. The pleasure of riding these open trolleys and other Connecticut Company cars can still be enjoyed at the Branford Trolley Museum. — *Norton D. Clark*

Third Avenue Railway System started as a horsecar operation between City Hall and 61st Street. By 1870, 1,700 horses were necessary to maintain the service. Conversion to cable cars started in 1885, followed by conversion to electricity beginning in 1899. The greatest growth came in 1898, when three other properties, including the Union Railway, were acquired. Union Railway, a consolidation of small properties, operated virtually all lines in the Bronx and lower Westchester County. In contrast to Manhattan, lines in the County had overhead wire, single track, side-of-road operation and fixed headways similar to a small town's operations. In 1945, car 387 has just crossed under the New York aqueduct. The final remnants of the Third Avenue Railway System operated in Yonkers until November, 1952. — *Charles A. Brown*

Originally an open platform car, 761 was one of ten cars built by American Car in 1898, for the Brooklyn Rapid Transit Co. It was rebuilt in 1923, and was still in service in October, 1943, on New Utrecht Avenue at 39th Street in Brooklyn. Sharp observers will note the wartime blackout device over the headlight. The characteristic front bay window was added around 1906, when BRT was ordered to install windbreaks for the protection of motormen. In 1923, Brooklyn Manhattan Transit Company arose in the reorganization of BRT. BMT quickly placed its surface operations into a newly formed affiliate, Brooklyn & Queens Transit Corp., a company well known for its introduction of the PCC car. Streetcar operations ceased on October 31, 1956; however, BMT's rapid transit operations continue as a part of the NYCTA. —*Norton D. Clark*

In September, 1956, only two Philadelphia Transportation Co. lines were still using the 1923 Brill double-ended 5200's. On an eastbound run on route 79, Snyder Avenue, car 5292 loads at the Snyder Avenue end of the Broad Street Subway. The track, carefully relaid just a few years before, had about six more weeks of use. Buses took over in October. When ordered in 1923, the 135 cars in this series were only part of the largest equipment acquisition program since between 1911 and 1913, when 1,500 of the well-known Near-Sides were ordered. The 1923 program also included 385 single end cars (8000-8384) and a number of workcars. Except for three cars, the entire fleet was scrapped between 1955 and 1957. Streetcar operations on former PTC lines are continued in 1978, by the Southeastern Pennsylvania Transportation Authority. — *Joseph M. Canfield*

A durable 1906 Stephenson-built coach loads Ocean City bound passengers at the Atlantic City and Shore Railroad's Virginia Avenue (Boardwalk) terminal. Car 113 was one of twenty cars that inaugurated electric service on the West Jersey & Shore's former steam dummy line from Atlantic City to Somers Point. AC&S was merely an operating company using Pennsylvania Road track. In 1907, completion of the trestle across the Great Egg Harbor River extended service to Ocean City. Crossing that trestle and the high-speed third rail equipped trackage combined for a memorable ride. In 1945, the line was sold to the Atlantic City Transprtation Co. The original cars survived a mid-twenties recommendation for replacement and the destruction by fire in 1946 of the trestle, only to roll their final miles in January, 1948. — *David H. Cope*

One of the so-called War Board cars, 6888 was originally destined for Birmingham, but instead was diverted from Brill's plant to Philadelphia for service on the Hog Island line. World War I had stimulated streetcar traffic in the industrial northeast, and finding enough cars to handle the increased traffic required special efforts. With the emergency over, the cars were surplus, and in May, 1923, four cars of this group were sold to Atlantic City. There they became 6885-6888. They were joined by 6889-6890, purchased new in 1923, and 6845-6850 which came from Philadelphia via the Ocean City Electric. The end was seventeen days away when, on December 11, 1955, car 6888 was en route from the Inlet loop over the private right-of-way that swept through a long curve onto Atlantic Avenue. Ahead is suburban Margate. — *David H. Cope*

There was an emotional appeal to the Red Arrow Lines out of proportion to its size. It was a remarkable suburban transportation company that reflected the pride of three generations of men named Merritt Taylor who led the company. The Philadelphia & West Chester Traction was both a city and suburban trolley and the Philadelphia & Western was a high-speed interurban. Combined as the Philadelphia Suburban Transportation Company, they were virtually the scope of electric railways in miniature. On August 3, 1941, the four types of cars that then served the surface system posed at Llanerch carbarn. With the exception of five Jewett-built cars (represented by car 42) the entire passenger roster consisted of "hometown" products from J. G. Brill Co. The occasion was the arrival of "Brilliners" 1-10, the very last cars built by Brill. — *James P. Shuman*

Though overshadowed by the fierce competition between Pennsy's West Jersey and Seashore, and Reading's Atlantic City Railroad steam trains across New Jersey WL&S's electric operations are worthy of note. When completed in 1906, it was the longest steam road electrification in North America. Stiff highway competition and the depression caused WJ&S to cut back electric service from Atlantic City's Tennessee Avenue depot before 1932, and to combine with ACR as the Pennsylvania-Reading Seashore Lines in 1933. The fleet of owl-eyed MU's continued hauling commuters from Millville to Camden. In 1948, shortly before the wood cars were condemned, a train pauses at Westville on the three track section that extended from Camden to Woodbury. Steam-powered trains replaced the remaining steel cars on September 26, 1949. — *David H. Cope*

Raymond Loewy's first commission from the Pennsylvania Railroad was to redesign trash cans in Penn Station; his second was the GG1. His concept of an unbroken shell welded to the frame saved millions of dollars in construction and maintenance costs, plus improved the appearance and aerodynamics of the locomotive. The GG1 evolved from operating the O1 and P5's, and testing a New Haven EP-3. The EP-3 had a 4-6+6-4 (2-C+C-2) wheel arrangement that rode well and was easy on track. When introduced in August, 1934, the GG1 used this arrangement, which gave the motor its name; Class G was a 4-6-0 steam engine on the PRR. At ease in freight or passenger service, the GG1 served all. During a coal strike in 1946, 4885 rests at Media, a place they did not regularly serve, after pulling a commuter train from Philadelphia. — *Charles A. Brown*

"G Motor" 4910 urges the southbound "Morning Congressional" through Crum Lynne, Pennsylvania, in September 1953, as the train maintains its mile-a-minute average scheduled speed for the 27 miles between Philadelphia and Wilmington. Of the 139 GG1's that were built, only six were repainted to the Tuscan livery coincident with re-equipping of the "Congo" and "The Senator" in 1952. The others retained their Bruns-wick green livery. Speed, riding qualities, and durability made the GG1 noteworthy. In tests, a GG1 and trailing coach reached 100 mph in 64.5 seconds from a dead stop, and 115 mph top speeds were often maintained. The motors developed 4620 continuous horsepower with a 9,000 hp short-time rating. There are three motor circuits with four motors each—a virtual multiple-unit train within a single chassis. — *Charles A. Brown*

From a base of city streetcar operations, Albert L. Johnson projected lines from Allentown to New York and Philadelphia. His early death in 1901 halted planning for the New York line, but service to Chestnut Hill soon followed. On December 12, 1912, a new high-speed line via Norristown to the P&W's 69th Street Terminal in Upper Darby opened with six 800-series interurban cars. Six more followed in July 1913, the same month that construction of a private car for charter service and official parties was authorized. From the smashed hulk of streetcar 159 arose car 999. Unfortunately, while official parties were many, revenue producing charters were few. Thus, in 1921, car 999 was rebuilt as coach 812. In August 1949, 812 is at Emaus Junction, just south of Allentown, on a charter to Philadelphia. — *David H. Cope*

In addition to the interurban line to Norristown, the Lehigh Valley Transit Company also operated city and suburban services on its line to Easton. In 1916, the purchase of twelve center entrance cars from Southern Car Company was approved. Their overall dimensions were influenced by private car 999, and they were designed to be a universal car, adaptable to both interurban, suburban and city services. Continued need for Philadelphia service and their slow acceleration and interurban dimensions precluded their universal use. Soon the center-entrances were closed and the sides of the cars were rebuilt. The series was ravaged during the Depression, and only 701, 702, 704 and 710 survived. In February 1943, car 704 passes through Souderton on yet another run between Allentown and Philadelphia over the famed "Liberty Bell Route." — *Charles A. Brown*

Reflecting the influences of Dr. Thomas Conway, this 1930 Cincinnati-built former Cincinnati & Lake Erie lightweight represents a radical departure in car design. Aluminum and steel construction allowed a low 24-ton weight, which when powered by 400 h.p. worth of motors achieved speeds, during tests, in excess of 80 mph. While not enough to save the C&LE, their availability allowed the LVT to modernize. Arriving late in 1938, they were welcomed as LVT deteriorated after the Depression. Some work was done on the cars, including removal of the front dash when the sheeting was renewed, addition of a back-up trolley for barn moves in Allentown and new horns. They resumed revenue service on February 13, 1939. On March 2, 1951, car 1001, ex-C&LE 128, is at Summit Lawn, having again conquered South Mountain. — *William D. Middleton*

Between July 1938 and January 1939, LVT received 43 second-hand cars from six different railways. The crown jewel was club car 1030, ex-Indiana Railroad 55. Built in 1931, its design was influenced by the C&LE cars. Resplendent in its new Mountain Ash Scarlet and Picador Cream livery, it was chartered by the Lehigh Valley Chapter of the National Railway Historical Society for a preview trip to Easton and Norristown on September 28, 1941. It is meeting Easton Limited car 1100, one of four former Dayton and Troy curved-side cars at Candy Factory Siding, Bethlehem. LVT rail service to Easton ended on August 15, 1949, and Philadelphia service was cut back to Norristown on September 24th. Total abandonment came eight hours after permission was received on September 6, 1951. Car 1030 is preserved at Seashore Trolley Museum. — *James P. Shuman*

Those youthful swimmers seem more interested in swimming than either the Laurel Line train or the magnificent wood roller coaster of Rocky Glen Park. Even at this late date, August 31, 1947, the Lackawanna & Wyoming Valley derived 60% of its revenue from passenger service. But receivership was a year away and passenger service ended on December 31, 1952. However, unlike most interurban lines, the Laurel Line was constructed to unusually high standards. What resulted was a line completely on a private right-of-way, with steam road clearances, with third rail except for the approach to Wilkes-Barre Terminal. This permitted interchange freight services with area railroads of sufficient volume that diesels took over freight operations in August 1953. The remaining trackage was conveyed to Conrail. — *James P. Shuman*

Scranton Terminal looks almost like a hobby shop window, particularly when one considers the number of railroads portrayed here that no longer exist. But on September 8, 1951, the L&WV was still very much in the passenger business with these fine Osgood-Bradley cars. Ahead lies the one mile tunnel through the hills of south Scranton, the crossing of Roaring Brook at the south portal, and the mostly double track line to Wilkes-Barre. This very scenic line crossed almost forty bridges, including the impressive 682-foot steel deck trestle over the Lehigh Valley and Delaware and Hudson railroads at Avoca. In 1903, the line's promoters conceived a 200-mile system in this populous anthracite country. The cost of this heavily graded line traversing the mountainous terrain in the Susquehanna River Valley stopped construction at Wilkes-Barre. — *George Krambles*

Scranton was also served by an extensive street railway system. Scranton Transit car 505 was one of ten cars built by Osgood-Bradley in 1929. The cars were called "Electromobiles". However, frequently they were incorrectly called Master Units, which were similar in appearance but built by Brill. These cars ran until December 18, 1954, when all service was abandoned. Scranton's trackage was rough at best, but due to deep cushioned leather seats the cars afforded a rather comfortable ride. On September 13, 1947, car 505 is at the end of the Green Ridge suburban line, Scranton's first and last line. Regular service began on December 1, 1886. Other lines were soon constructed so at one time a person could ride from Forest City to Hazleton. At the end, the system had dwindled down to its original line to Green Ridge Street. — *Norton D. Clark*

On April 20, 1941, two Wilkes-Barre Railways cars are ready to leave Sans Souci Park Junction on the Nanticoke line for Hanover. The regular service car, 760, was built in 1924 by Brill for the East Penn Traction of Pottsville. Nine years later, it would be the final car to operate to Hanover. Behind 760 is car 356, a 1911 Brill product that was one of 30 cars purchased in the 1911-1913 improvement program. Car 356 will operate as a second section on the three mile run to Hanover. Hanover was really a branch off the Nanticoke line which operated from the Square in Wilkes-Barre to Nanticoke, 15 miles southwest of town. These two lines were the final street railway operation of a system that at one time consisted of over 100 route miles. The final conversion to bus was on October 14, 1950. — *James P. Shuman*

In "The Electric Interurban Railway in America", authors Hilton and Due note the opposition of eastern steam railroads to the crossing of their tracks by those of electric railways. For example, a trolley ride between Philadelphia and Harrisburg was possible by either of two routes, but both were interrupted by walks across Reading Company tracks. On the northerly route, via Reading, there were two such breaks, one each at Ephrata and Boyertown, while on the southern route via Downington the break was at Coatsville. Regardless of the route, one rode the Hershey Transit Company to complete the journey. On June 23, 1940, the last day of service to Elizabethtown, car 1 is at Deodate. This 1904 Brill classic was built for predecessor Hummelstown and Campbelltown Street Railway. The last car ran on December 21, 1946. — *John D. Siebert*

If one took the southern route to Harrisburg, they would have ridden on Conestoga Traction Co. In 1910, this was one of Pennsylvania's major systems as 160 miles of route radiated from Lancaster's Penn Square. Thirteen years later, the electric railway industry had good cause for celebration. Costs appeared to be stabilizing following the abnormal postwar period. The number of companies entering receivership in 1923 was the lowest in over a decade, while the amount of rolling stock ordered was the greatest since 1913. Of the 4029 vehicles ordered in 1923, CT ordered 17 passenger cars, five of which were Cincinnati curved-side cars, series 65-69, delivered in June 1924. The final car of CT's group is at Country Club stop on the Ephrata line on August 10, 1941. CT's cars bowed to buses on September 21, 1947. — *John D. Siebert*

The street railway companies in Hagerstown and Frederick merged as the Hagerstown & Frederick on April 17, 1913. The resulting 87-mile system was the largest in Maryland. It included the 17-mile system from Frederick north to Thurmont, which opened to service on October 11, 1908, as the Washington, Frederick & Gettysburg. What resulted was an incredibly pastoral trolley line. Its longevity was due to freight traffic and the pro-tective umbrella of the mighty parent that the railway spawned, Potomac Edison Company. On May 18, 1941, the sole Cincinnati-built car on the H&F roster poses on Rudy's Hollow bridge near Middletown, Maryland during a NRHS excursion to Hagerstown. But it was not to last; the Hagerstown line was abandoned in two pieces during 1947, and service to Thurmont ended on February 20, 1954. — *James P. Shuman*

Electric railways were often affiliated with utility companies. The vast Virginia Electric Power Co. had railway operations in many southeastern Virginia cities. One of the divisions was Norfolk. But even the mighty purchased equipment from the small. The Westside Electric Street Railway and the Webster, Monessen, Belle Vernon and Fayette City Street Railway operated out of Charleroi, Pennsylvania. The two lines were jointly oper-ated and each ordered three identical cars from Kuhlman in 1926. Pittsburgh Railways operated the lines from 1929 to 1933, subsequently selling the Kuhlmans to the Lehigh Valley Transit. LVT never used the cars and in turn resold them in 1939 to VEPCO, which assigned them to the Norfolk Division. VEPCO 702 is in South Norfolk on August 25, 1941. It was originally WESR 251. — *John D. Siebert*

With its siderods rhythmically clanking and white flags flapping, Virginian Railway EL3A set 106 heads a westbound manifest out of Blacksburg Tunnel on July 18, 1956. Located near Merrimac, Virginia, this tunnel was just 30 miles from the eastern end of the 134 mile electrified Third Sub-Division between Roanoke and Mullens. West Virginia coal was the basic reason for the Virginian's existence. However, before 1925, moving that coal eastbound from Mullens up 2% grades to cross the Cumberland plateau at Clark's Gap reduced steam engines of that era to plodding giants. The solution was electrification. Twelve three-unit electric locomotives were delivered by Westinghouse in 1925. Known as the ''Squareheads'', they moved coal up the mountains at 14 mph, compared to steam locomotives moving at 7 mph. — *James P. Shuman*

Looking down from the Norfolk and Western's Cambria to Blacksburg Branch bridge provides a good vantage point for action of the Virginian. On this July 1956 day an eastbound coal extra halts to receive orders from the block operator at Merrimac. The big General Electric locomotive is one of four two-unit sets delivered in 1948. These locomotives had motor generators which converted the 11,000 volt, 25 cycle, AC power into DC power for the traction motors. Their performance convinced the Virginian to retain the electrification. Replacement of the "Squareheads" was completed with delivery of twelve rectifier locomotives in 1956. However, the consolidation of the Virginian into the N & W in 1959 made the end inevitable as loads moved east on the Virginia and empties returned via the N & W. The last electric ran on June 20, 1962. — *James P. Shuman*

In 1978, standardization of transit vehicle design occupies much of the industry's attention. Yet between 1922 and 1929, Cincinnati Car Company delivered 400 lightweight, curved-side cars which became known as the ''Rubber Stamp Trolley''. Perhaps the most atypical cars of this design were delivered to Georgia Power Company's Atlanta Northern in 1926. These ten cars were equipped with multiple-unit control, and were the only curved-sides that had train doors. They served on the A-N's lines to Marietta and Stone Mountain. The Marietta line was interesting, as fares were collected when leaving the car northbound and entering the car southbound. The schedule was so tight that it was necessary to use two men on the ''one-man'' cars on the north end of the line to collect fares.
— *William C. Janssen*

Traffic counts soared during World War II due to gas rationing and completion of the Bell Bomber plant. For its interurban lines, Georgia Power acquired more curved-sides: three from the Nashville-Franklin, and six from the Toledo & Indiana. For train service, the T & I cars were equipped with Tomlinson couplers from the Chicago Surface Lines and PC control. Among the cars acquired for the city lines was 644, which posed shortly after its arrival. It was one of fifteen multiple unit cars built for Erie, Pennsylvania in 1923. The infrequently used MU controls were removed by Erie in 1925, and by May, 1935, the Erie system was converted to bus. The cars were stored until sold to Atlanta in 1942. City service and the Marietta line ended in 1947, and the last car to Stone Mountain operated on April 10, 1949. — *William C. Janssen*

Indiana Service Corporation achieved a modern design with ten streetcars built by St. Louis Car Co. in 1917. Subsequent orders into the mid-twenties put the Fort Wayne system into the forefront of modernized transit properties. However, by 1940, ISC felt the further modernization of its transit system meant replacing streetcars with trolley buses. Thus, several routes were converted on July 7, 1940. With a contracted system, there were surplus cars in Ft. Wayne, several of which were sold to other properties. Shortly after its arrival in 1942, ex-ISC car 506 is serving the Municipal Railways of St. Petersburg, Florida, as car 119. Together with car 118, former Indiana Service Corporation 507, they were a pleasant contrast to the wooden seat double-truck Birneys that were used in St. Petersburg. — *William C. Janssen*

In 1918, the Hershey Sugar Company built a 58-mile interurban railway from Casa Blanca, a port city across the bay from Havana, eastward to Matanzas. Sixty years later, it continues to be operated in the traditional methods of a U. S. interurban. Even more incredible, its future seems secure. The principal purpose for building the line was to move sugar. Thus, freight service has always been significant. Hershey Cuban sixty-ton freight motors 23 and 27, built by General Electric in 1920 and 1926, respectively, power train number 52 the eastbound mainline time freight at Justiz, 13 miles east of Casa Blanca, on November 23, 1956. Ahead is Central Hershey, the focal point of the line, where the railway's shops and offices were located as well as the parent company's sugar mill. These locomotives still operate in 1978. — *George Krambles*

A ride to Matanzas begins on the narrow street of the noisy waterfront of Casa Blanca. The interurban cars were built by Brill in 1921, and were constructed with steel underframes and side sheathing up to the beltrails. Above the beltrail, oak and pine was used with mahogany interior finish. Our train, consisting of coach 109 and a 200-series combine pauses at Guanabo, 15 miles from Casa Blanca and halfway to Central Hershey.

The eastern end of the line beyond Central Hershey offers increasingly better scenery, including occasional views of the Atlantic Ocean, jungle-like vegetation, steep grades, rock cuts and the breathtaking Yumuri Valley just before entering Matanzas. In 1978, these cars rebuilt with arch roofs and steel sheathing still ply the railroad. Further, the long-sought access to Central Havana appears to be in sight. — *George Krambles*

In addition to its mainline passenger service, Hershey Cuban operates a number of branch line schedules centered on the great sugar mill at Central Hershey. Most of this service was geared to work shifts at the mill and many, according to a timetable footnote, operated only when the refinery did. Car 213, built by Cincinnati Car Co. in 1922, stands in the street outside of the Central Hershey Mill on a June 1957 afternoon after completing the single daily round trip scheduled over the Bainoa branch as train numbers 18 and 21. This branch line was interesting, as the 1200-volt DC electrification extends only Bainoa. Beyond the interurbans are towed by diesels to Central San Antonio. These little Cincinnati's have been scrapped, but their trucks and electrical gear now power converted former East German diesel railcars. — *William D. Middleton*

Birmingham, the "Pittsburgh of the South," had city and interurban operations similar to Pittsburgh, but while that city modernized with a large fleet of PCC's, Birmingham took a different course of action. Between 1926 and 1947, the Birmingham Electric Company purchased no new cars. Instead, the company acquired second-hand cars from a multitude of cities. Car 547, a Cincinnati Car Co. curved-side car, was originally Stark Electric Railroad (Alliance to Canton, Ohio) car 47. Owing to the riding customs then used in the south, the car was rebuilt in a Peter Witt style by Perley A. Thomas & Co. Eight cars, 541-548, were purchased from Stark in 1939 and they ran principally on the suburban runs to Tarrant City and North and South Bessemer until 1952. They were among the last conventional cars to operate in Birmingham. — *Gordon E. Lloyd*

With its variety of equipment, Birmingham was a virtual museum. Along with the unusual and wonderful collection of revenue cars, Birmingham's service car fleet was equally interesting. The group included the usual sprinklers, cranes and differential dump cars plus such oddities as cement cars, weed burners and this diminutive rail grinder. From its construction in the company shops in 1928 until the arrival of the Pullman trackless trolleys in 1946 it was numbered 123. Along with the other utility cars, it was then renumbered into the 2000 series. Car 2123 retained this number until it was scrapped in 1953. Before dawn on Sunday, April 20, 1953, PCC 812 made the final streetcar run when it closed out service on the Ensley Line. The 48 PCC cars were sold to Toronto, their 4700-series, who resold 19 of the cars to Philadelphia in 1976. — *Gordon E. Lloyd*

Col. J. F. Strickland, started in the public utility business and in 1905, he began promoting the Texas Traction Company between Dallas and Sherman to connect with the Denison and Sherman Railway into Denison. By 1911, both Strickland and Stone and Webster Engineering Company of Boston were planning lines south from Dallas to Waxahachie. Ultimately, Strickland prevailed. His Southern Traction Company completed lines to Corsicana and Waco. Texas Traction and Southern Traction merged as the Texas Electric Railway on January 31, 1917. However, they were operated as two distinct lines due to Texas Traction being at 600-volt potential, while Southern Traction was at 1200 volts. On July 3, 1948, car 320 is at the Southern Pacific crossing in Waxahachie. On New Year's Eve that year the trains stopped running. — *George Krambles*

Charles Page was born in Wisconsin, worked for the Northern Pacific and made his fortune as an Oklahoma oilman. A philanthropist, he funded construction of the Sand Springs Home for Orphans and Widows. Unhappy with the steam road passenger service, he built the Sand Springs Railway in 1911 to assure dependable transportation between Tulsa and the home. He also contributed the railroad to the home as a continuing source of income. Electrification came a few years later and in 1934 the line acquired five of the seven pioneering lightweight cars built for the Cincinnati, Lawrenceburg and Aurora in 1918. In the 1940's car 66 is looping in Sand Springs. When passenger service ended on January 3, 1955, all but one of these cars had been scrapped. Sister car 68 is preserved at the Illinois Railway Museum. — *Frank E. Butts*

Electric railways operated in Oklahoma before that territory became a state. Operations of the Metropolitan Street Railway Company began on February 7, 1903, and the Oklahoma territory became the 46th state on November 16, 1907. By 1913 all of the city and interurban lines operating in Oklahoma City were under the control of Oklahoma Railways. Service was provided by a variety of equipment, the appearance of some which could be charitably described as utilitarian. Modernization of the city lines began with the purchase of thirty safety cars in 1929 and 1930. The program was continued when ten 1927 Kuhlman-built cars used by the Eastern Michigan Railway in Flint were purchased late in 1936. Car 141, formerly EM 3250, is running on Grand Avenue in front of the interurban terminal. Cars were also acquired from Rockford, Illinois.—*Frank E. Butts*

Interurban services were also modernized. The terminal was extensively remodeled in 1928 and was used by local and interurban cars as well as buses in later days. Lightweight interurban cars were purchased from among others, the Fort Wayne—Lima operation of Indiana Service Corporation. Car 221 was one of the former Ft. Wayne—Lima cars. It was heavily used during World War II. At the outset of the conflict a Naval training station was opened in Norman. The resulting volume of traffic necessitated the construction of a loop to replace the pre-existing wye. In addition freight equipment was rebuilt for passenger use and several more second-hand cars were added to the roster. At the cessation of hostilities, passenger traffic fell sharply. The last runs came shortly after this January 30, 1947 scene. — *James P. Shuman*

Union Electric Railway of Kansas could best be described as being held together by chewing gum and bailing wire. The line wandered for 77 miles from Parsons, Kansas to Nowata, Oklahoma. A trip over the entire line, which probably no one except the hardiest of railfans ever took, consumed four hours. On February 1, 1947, Car 70 is about to leave Parsons for a 52-mile trip to reach Coffeyville, Kansas. By contrast, the competing rail-road service traversed a 31-mile route between these two towns. Leaving Parsons the interurban first went west, then south and finally east to reach Coffeyville. On the way one might have to help chase wandering bovines off the tracks—tracks that had seen precious little maintenance thus giving both the car and its riders a good shaking as they stumbled along. Mercifully, abandonment came on April 4, 1948. — *James P. Shuman*

The very creation of the Union Electric must be questioned as the population of none of the towns on the railway ever exceeded 15,000. Lightweight cars were utilized as an economy measure. However, the ride, particularly on the single truck cars, must have been excruciating. No frogs were utilized at crossings—the rails were simply mitered and butted together. Propulsion power was provided by a gas fired main generator. Finally, revenues covered operating expenses in only two of the 26 years that the line operated. No wonder! A one cent-a-mile tariff effected in 1935 was still valid five years later as evidenced by the hand lettered dash sign on Birney Car 17. On March 23, 1940, this car, one of three assigned to city service in Independence, is on the Cement Plant Line in that city. Local service was also provided in Coffeyville. — *Frank E. Butts*

An energetic easterner William B. Strang arrived in Kansas City. By 1905 he had organized two companies: The Strang Land Company and the Kansas City, Olathe, Lawrence and Topeka Electric Railway. Only the 21 miles from Kansas City to Olathe was constructed and the railroad, more commonly known among the local residents as the "Strang Line," was renamed the Missouri & Kansas Interurban Railway. The line commenced service with a gasoline motor of Strang's design which, of course, was called the "Strang Car." Electrification followed in 1909. Service was provided by a group of classic wood cars. Thirty years later, Car 115 one of the six original motor cars is in downtown Olathe. For a town with less than 4,000 inhabitants all those autos were not a good omen for continued railway service. — *Frank E. Butts*

120

The fortunes of the Missouri & Kansas were never good. But they took a turn for the worse on February 11, 1925. On that day the carbarn and powerhouse in Overland Park were completely destroyed by fire. Four of the wood motor cars and the three trailers were consumed. Two motors, stored overnight at the Olathe terminal survived. These two cars and leased Kansas City streetcars maintained service. With speed that would cause today's car buyers to envy, American Car Co. delivered three lightweight steel cars in August. One of these cars, Car 118, is in Olathe in 1939. The line was not to last much longer. Passenger service ended on July 9, 1940. On July 25th the morning freight had found 1500 feet of trolley wire stolen the night before . . . the train never reached Olathe and the railroad was abandoned. — *Frank E. Butts*

Beginning in 1868, separate companies provided street railway service in Omaha and in Council Bluffs. A successor company combined the operations, constructed a bridge over the Missouri River and electrified. In 1902 further corporate simplifications brought all the underlying subsidiaries into one company, the Omaha and Council Bluffs Street Railway. In later years, despite the common ownership, operations on each side of the river were distinctive. Council Bluffs local service was provided by Birneys. Omaha local service was provided by steel double truck cars like home-built 1004, seen here in Omaha on June 23, 1952. Intercity service was provided by wooden double truck cars. Streetcar operations terminated in Council Bluffs on September 25, 1948 and in Omaha on March 6, 1955. — *Gordon E. Lloyd*

Since 1904 the Cedar Rapids and Iowa City Railway had utilized a small group of exceptionally well maintained wood cars. In 1939 six cars were purchased from the Cincinnati and Lake Erie. Their high-performance characteristics earned them the name ''Yellow Comets'', and their propensity to roll at speed the motto ''Swing and sway the Crandic way''. With the arrival of car 120 from the Indiana Railroad the quintessence of light-weight high-speed interurban car design could be found on a single 27-mile railway. On May 7, 1944, the cars meet in Iowa City. They served until the end of passenger service on May 30, 1953. Car 120, Illinois Railway Museum's first acquisition, is preserved as IR 65, Car 118 is at Seashore Trolley Museum, and Car 116 has been restored to its C & LE appearance by the Ohio Railway Museum. — *Charles A. Brown*

Iowa was well known as land of the "steam road trolleys". The lines were built to steam railroad standards and some, like the Waterloo, Cedar Falls and Northern, at one time were operated by steam. For several reasons, the WCF&N was the favorite of many; first, its passenger service outlasted the other Iowa lines—until February 20, 1956; second, the railway was genuinely accommodating to fans, and finally, its equipment was dis-tinctive. WCF&N's two open platform observation cars were certainly distinctive, but even the lightly patronized Waverly line had its own car. In 1936, car 141 was rebuilt to replace wood car 34 as the "Waverly car". Car 141 is pictured at Denver, Iowa on September 14, 1942. The lack of need for passenger seats is attested by the reason for the stop—express business! — *Charles A. Brown*

Two ladies have alighted from a Rock Island Lines' train at Marble Rock, Iowa, and are making the connection with Charles City Western's car 53 on May 6, 1944. CCW's line ran from Marble Rock, Iowa, population 700, through Charles City to Colwell, population 100. As a result, there were never more than two passenger runs per day and they were scheduled to connect with the Rock Island trains. Car 53, which came from the Shore Line Electric of Connecticut, together with car 50 provided this casual passenger service that included the motorman talking with passengers at their seats as the car rolled along. The reason for the line was the significant freight operations in Charles City, population 9,000, a manufacturing town that is still served by CCW's successor, the dieselized Charles City Division of the Iowa Terminal Railroad. — *Charles A. Brown*

The expert car building accomplishments of Twin City Rapid Transit Company's 31st Street (Nicollet) Shops are legend. Among its last cars was 1216, which was built in 1906. Thirty years later, Nicollet's successor, Snelling Shops, was assigned to rebuild several of the "standard" cars for one-man service, including some of TCRT's "suburban" cars, which were really interurbans. They operated west from Minneapolis on the Lake Minnetonka lines and northeast from St. Paul on the Stillwater Division. In September 1951, car 1216 is at Mahtomedi, a branch off the Stillwater line along the east side of White Bear Lake. In just two months the interurban line would be abandoned; however, car 1216 served until the end of streetcar service on June 18, 1954. In 1978, sister car 1300 is operated by the Minnesota Transportation Museum. — *George Krambles*

A little beyond the Canadian border on the far northwestern side of Lake Superior is the city of Thunder Bay, home of Hawker Siddeley, a major manufacturer of rail vehicles. In days past, Thunder Bay was two separate municipalities; Port Arthur and Fort William, and public transit services were provided by separate companies. For many years the Port Arthur Public Utilities Commission ran a delightful assortment of single and double truck wooden cars. Car 70 is behind the car house posed on the ladder track on Van Horne Street. This little beauty had been in the barn, but an accommodating employee brought it outside for the photographer on this day in July of 1941. At this time the company owned 19 passenger cars and two snow plows. Rail service terminated on February 15, 1948. — *Frank E. Butts*

Fort William Utilities boasted a grand union at Victoria and Syndicate. Westbound car 45 is about to pound this special work in July 1941. The two cities were connected by the "Main Line" route. Through cars to and from Port Arthur operated down Simpson Street to Victoria. Rail service ended on October 15, 1947, but bus service was maintained by each city until that December when a through-routed trolley bus again connected the two cities until 1955. However, back in 1941, Fort William's roster was as varied as Port Arthur's. There were 21 passenger cars, including four trailers, three of which were from the same series of Cleveland Railway's cars pictured in South Bend on page 37 of this book. The motors included cars from Winnipeg and Cincinnati curved-side cars from the Northampton Transit of Easton, Pennsylvania. — *Frank E. Butts*

With the exception of two home-built cars, Winnipeg Electric Railway's last new cars arrived in 1920. In the mid-twenties conversion to one-man operations caused major rebuilding of the fleet. In the case of the 700-series, the cars were "turned" end-for-end. As built these cars had double doors at the rear. Thus the rear became the front so there could be entry and exit adjacent to the operator's position. On May 20, 1951, four years before service ended on September 21, 1955, car 706 traverses the pleasant reserved right-of-way, that was acquired with the acquisition of two inter-urban properties, leading up Broadway from the Canadian National Railway station. Such rights-of-way explain the reason for the high boxy appearance of earlier Winnipeg cars. Sturdy cars were deemed necessary to buck drifting snow on open track. — *William E. Robertson*

Usually steam railroads did not construct trolley systems, but the Colorado & Southern (now the Burlington Northern) did so in Fort Collins, Colorado. In 1907, C&S subsidiary Denver & Interurban Railway began operations. Bankruptcy and a surprise end of service came in 1918. In May 1919, a new company, Fort Collins Municipal Railway, resumed service. Its riders were pleased with the fleet of Birneys that served until the end, June 30, 1951. These cars were the last regularly scheduled Birneys in North America. The last car to operate, number 22, which is preserved at Colorado Railway Museum, is laying over in the three-way downtown intersecton of Mountain Avenue, Linden Street and College Avenue. Every twenty minutes the three operating cars in town would pass simultaneously on each leg of the wye. — *Donald Duke*

Denver Tramways served the "Mile High City" and its two subsidiaries provided interurban services. The Denver and Northwestern headed northwest to Arvada where one branch continued to Leyden while the other went west to Golden. Like Tramways, this line had narrow gauge (3' 6") track. The other interurban was the standard gauge Denver & Intermountain Railroad which went straight west to Golden. Only five cars were needed for this service, which was essentially a suburban trolley. Two of these cars, 818 and 819, were built by the Tramways as a part of a 20-car order in 1922 and converted to standard gauge in 1924. On February 26, 1950, those two cars are at Devinny siding (Wadsworth Boulevard), the place where the two cars in-service on the line usually met. Conversion to bus came about three months later, on June 3rd. — *George Krambles*

Few shared Simon Bamberger's optimism for a "local" railway between Salt Lake City and Ogden until Mormon leader Brigham Young endorsed the idea. Construction started in 1892 and reached Farmington in 1895. Just to the north was a large swamp where the railroad created an artificial lake and built a grand amusement park that was named Lagoon. The park attracted considerable summer traffic—so much that six high-seating capacity trailers numbered 350-355 were delivered in 1916. When rebuilt around 1920, the cars were closed and motorized. The unusual ridges on the side of the car were caused by using the steel lining of a mining flume to sheath the car. Just six days before rail passenger service ended, car 354 pauses at Lagoon on August 31, 1952. Due to their 84-seat capacity these cars were the workhorses of the railroad. —*George Krambles*

The Salt Lake & Ogden Railway finally reached Ogden in 1908, but steam powered trains continued until electric operations commenced on May 28, 1910. Eighteen motors and six trailers, built by Jewett and Niles, attracted considerable new traffic and reminded Utah residents of the Bamberger family. In 1917, Simon Bamberger became Utah's governor, his son Julian succeeded him at the railway and the line's public nickname was officially adopted. Under Julian's leadership "The Bamberger Electric Railroad" constantly rebuilt its original wood cars, many of which survived the entire 42 years of electric operation. The line's only all-steel cars, 125-129, arrived in 1939. They were five highspeed Brill "Bullets" built in 1932 for the Fonda Johnstown & Gloversville. On May 12, 1951, car 127 is in Farmington. — *James P. Shuman*

The color scheme and oversize lettering do little to enhance the stark lines of this 1918-built McGuire-Cummings car. But considering the despair of Saltair Pavilion this may have been the only way to attire the six cars of this series. These low speed cars plied the 16-mile arrow straight line between the City and the Great Salt Lake. They were used as locomotives to haul home-built open trail cars jammed with passengers or carloads of freight. (The line's one and only locomotive was purchased used in 1946.) Saltair had no affiliations or connection with the other Utah interurbans. In fact, it competed with Bamberger for resort traffic (Lagoon vs. Saltair). On August 16, 1951, the electric operations gave way to diesels; however, cars 501 and 502 and the open trailers survived until 1959, when the final passenger train operated. — *Donald Duke*

In 1913 the Milwaukee Road announced plans to electrify parts of its Pacific Extension. The earliest operations began in the Great Falls, Montana yard in August 1915. When completed, the 3,000-volt D.C. electrification crossed five mountain ranges and covered 441 miles of the Rocky Mountain Division between Harlowton, Montana and Avery, Idaho, and 218 miles of the Coast Division between Othello and Seattle-Tacoma, Washington. Trains were moved by 42 of these 2-unit 1915 vintage GE locomotives like E42A, which is traversing the Bitter Root Mountains near Saltese in western Montana, during June 1956. They served into the 1970's. The first electric left Deer Lodge for Three Forks on December 1, 1915 and almost 59 years later the last electric arrived in Deer Lodge from Harlowton on June 15, 1974. — *George Krambles*

Montana's last street railway was the Electric Railway and Light Department of Anaconda Copper Mining Company or simply Anaconda Street Railway. From inception in 1890, its principal purpose was to carry workers to and from the smelter. Even the workers' labor contract provided that a man had reported for work when he boarded the train. ASR operated four and five car trains at shift changes. Between rush periods, single cars operated in Anaconda and eastward between mountains of slag to the town of Opportunity. The original single-truck cars started to give way to double truck cars when number 10 arrived from St. Louis Car Co. in 1901. By 1915, when car 15 arrived, there were seven similar motors and six trailers. On September 4, 1950, car 15 is in Anaconda. Buses took over on December 31, 1951. — *George Krambles*

On May 28, 1951, three electric railways could be seen from this vantage point. On top of the slag pile, third-rail powered switchers are at work. In the foreground an ASR train heads toward the smelter. Between them an empty ore train is returning to the mines at Butte over the Butte, Anaconda & Pacific. In 1891, a bitter freight rate dispute led to building the BA&P. The line opened in 1893, to connect the mines, Milwaukee Road and Northern Pacific in Butte with the smelter in Anaconda. On Septermber 30, 1913, the 2400-volt DC electrification was energized. BA&P's traffic increased and more locomotives were ordered until 28 boxcabs were on the property. A processing plant in Butte eliminated the haul to Anaconda, and following a strike in 1967, diesels pulled the remaining trains as they continue to do in 1978. — *George Krambles*

One could leave Anaconda and travel for miles behind electric locomotives. BA&P's two passenger locomotives could only be discerned by their dual headlights and second pantograph. However, the Milwaukee Road had distinctive passenger locomotives on each division. Baldwin-Westinghouse built ten single-unit box cabs in 1920 for use on the Rocky Mountain Division. For 200 miles across Montana, the Milwaukee and Northern Pacific operated side-by-side. It was in this territory that the EP-3's paced NP's steam locomotives. The two railroads crossed at Sappington 60 miles east of Butte, where, on Saturday, May 30, 1953, motor E-10 leads the *Columbian*. It was the "milk train" in this territory, making several flag stops while the *Olympian* served only the major stops. By 1957 the EP-3's were the first class of motors to be retired. — *George Krambles*

They were so quiet that engineers rang the motor's bell frequently to announce their presence. Five of these unique motors were built by ALCO-GE in 1919 to haul passenger trains on the Coast Division. Named for their design, Bi-polar, the wheels of these steel centipedes were turned by axle-mounted armatures, thus eliminating gears and the resulting noise. Much publicity heralded their building, including shoving contests with steam locomotives at GE's plant, Kent, Washington and a curving trestle in the Cascades. Over 40 years of yeoman service were to follow. On September 7, 1950, E2 has run around the westbound *Olympian Hiawatha* in Seattle's Union station for the backward haul to Tacoma. After 1957, they served the Rocky Mountain Division. All except E2, now at the National Museum of Transport, were scrapped in 1962. — *George Krambles*

Great Northern's original line crossed the Cascade summit with a series of switchbacks and 4% grades. This trek was eliminated when a 2.63 mile tunnel was completed in 1900. In 1909 a short 6600 volt, three phase, AC electrification was placed in service. Four locomotives were purchased and were capable of grinding through the tunnel at a maximum speed of 15 miles per hour. To achieve further grade and curve reductions, the GN planned another tunnel which entered service on January 12, 1929—the 7.79 mile Cascade Tunnel. Between 1927 and 1930, ALCO-GE constructed eight of these motor-generator locomotives. Three of the big 63 foot, 260 ton motors move tonnage in May 1953. After a quarter century of service on the GN, they were sold to the Pennsylvania Railroad where they were used in helper service until 1962. — *George Krambles*

With the opening of the Cascade Tunnel, GN converted to a 11,000-volt, single phase AC system. Seventy-four route miles between Skykomish and Wenatchee, Washington, were electrified. All of the locomotives were motor-generator units which converted the AC trolley voltage into DC power which was fed to the traction motors. Motors 5000 A-B and 5002 A-B were delivered as single units while 5004 A-B, 5006 A-B and 5008 A-B were delivered as paired units by Baldwin-Westinghouse between 1926 and 1928. On June 13, 1956, 5004 A-B are moving through Peshastin, 19 miles west of Wenatchee. Improved tunnel ventilation and the diesel locomotive combined to render the relatively short electrified section an operating impediment. The last electric ran in August 1956 and these motors were scrapped. — *George Krambles*

In 1891, the New Westminster and Vancouver Tramways, Ltd. began operations. Its successor, British Columbia Electric Railway, used the Tramway's Central Park Line as the nucleus for Canada's longest interurban, the 76-mile run to Chilliwack. Daily except Sunday, a train departed Carrall Street Station, Vancouver, at 8:00 a.m. for the morning trip to Chilliwack. If traffic was heavy, the express car left early and would join the train at New Westminster. But such was not the case on September 7, 1950, 21 days before the service to Chilliwack ended, when home-built express motor 1700 heads the train at Central Park. At New Westminster, a division point, a new crew would carry on through the beautiful Fraser River Valley. Following lunch at Chilliwack, the train would leave for the return trip at 1:30 p.m. — *George Krambles*

BCER also operated an extensive street railway system in Vancouver, which in fine weather featured daily operation of open sightseeing cars. In addition BCER scheduled dense suburban service on 20-minute base headways between Vancouver and New Westminster over the Central Park Line. All of this was in marked contrast to the scheduled service beyond to Chilliwack that for years carded only three runs each way, an unusually spare schedule for any interurban. In May 1952, Kuhlman-built car 1308 grinds to a halt at Collingswood station while on a typical suburban trip over the Central Park Line. Service beyond Vancouver's city limits terminated on October 23, 1953. BCER's final passenger run was between Marpole and Steveston on February 28, 1958. In 1978 much of the railroad is operated by British Columbia Hydro. — *George Krambles*

Two interurbans served the fertile fruit-growing region of south-central Washington. In 1978 the Yakima Valley Transportation Company, a Union Pacific Railroad subsidiary, continues to use electric freight motors. Since 1976 YVT also hosts an antique trolley operation, a Bicentennial project that continues weekend operation with two single-truck cars built in Oporto, Portugal with Brill parts. Not as well known is the Walla Walla Valley Railway Company, a subsidiary of the Northern Pacific (now Burlington Northern) that operates twelve miles of railroad between Walla Walla, Washington and Milton-Freewater, Oregon. In the summer of 1949, freight motor 19 is making up its train in Walla Walla before leaving on its short journey into Oregon. Diesels replaced the electric motors in 1950. — *Robert T. McVay*

Portland Traction Company's line to Portland Heights and Council Crest was one of the most scenic rides in the United States. Reaching nearly 1,000 feet above downtown Portland, the line climbed a private right-of-way through a wooded park that afforded views of the Willamette and Columbia river valleys to the west and north as well as the virgin forest extending east to Mt. Hood. Brill semi-convertible cars equipped with magnetic brakes served this line that had approximately 70 curves, grades as steep as 12%, and safety derails placed at several points along the line. In September, 1949, car 509 serves the remnant of the line remaining in Portland Heights. A few weeks earlier on August 10, car 504 made the last run over the Council Crest loop. Final runs of all Portland streetcars came on February 26, 1950. — *George Krambles*

What is a true interurban and the longest continuously operated electrified railway is often debated. The first line of importance, East Side Railway, a predecessor of Portland Traction, began service on February 16, 1893. On August 25, 1949, car 1093 passes the Portland freight yard while serving this line to Oregon City. When PT's service ended in 1958, it was clearly the longest continuous interurban operation. By 1978 that had changed.

The Iowa Terminal Railroad's Mason City Division began operations on July 4, 1897 and remains electrified. As to passenger service, the Philadelphia & Western, now part of SEPTA, began service on May 22, 1907, and the Chicago South Shore & South Bend, whose predecessor operated a 3-mile streetcar line in East Chicago, Indiana, by September 1903, began regular interurban service on September 6, 1908. — *Robert T. McVay*

On May 30, 1951, car 4007 was serving its third owner as it traveled near Milwaukie, Oregon. Along with sister 4006, it was delivered in 1925 by Cincinnati Car Co. to the Albany & Southern Railroad. Four years later, that line was abandoned and the two cars were sold to the neighboring Fonda, Johnstown & Gloversville Railroad, where they served until abandonment in 1938. In that year, Portland Electric Power Co., Portland Traction's predecessor, had petitioned for abandonment; however, a plan developed by shippers and riders saved the line. Six city cars from the Indiana Railroad and 4006 and 4007 were purchased to modernize the car fleet. More cars were subsequently purchased from Yakima Valley, Key System and Pacific Electric. Thus, there was a virtual museum when passenger service was abruptly terminated on January 25, 1958. — *George Krambles*

In 1978, San Francisco is the only city west of the Mississippi River, except for the antique trolley in Yakima, Washington and a one-mile privately owned parking lot shuttle in Ft. Worth, Texas, that has streetcar service. In the Golden Gate city, Municipal Railways was created in 1909 to compete with the then dominant United Railways. What was to become the most successful car design in the city was introduced in 1913 when American Car delivered 65 modified California type cars to URR. When these cars were 12 years old, Muni made its first attempt to acquire URR's successor, Market Street Railway, a goal that was finally achieved in 1944. MSR's 200-series became Muni's 600-series. One of these cars, 606, leaves the Ferry Building on a 8/Market Street run on August 14, 1947, three years before its retirement. — *Robert T. McVay*

East Bay had a network of electric railways, comprised of the Interurban Electric Railway, Key System and Sacramento Northern, that the Bay Area Rapid Transit (BART) only partially replaces. Five cars survived the 1940 abandonment of SN's interurban service, as they were conveyed to the California State Toll Authority as collateral for the Authority equipping all of SN's cars with the Bay Bridge's automatic train control system.

Key System bought the five cars for scrap prices and placed them in rush hour service on the "F Line" thus earning them the nickname, "City of Berkeley." On August 11, 1947, car 496 leads the morning trip into East Bay Terminal. Car 495 is preserved as SN 1005 by the California Railway Museum. Key System, which assumed some of IER's lines upon its abandonment in 1941, ceased operations in 1958. — *Robert T. McVay*

Charlie Chaplin, Laurel and Hardy, and a host of others presented Los Angeles Railway's Type B cars to the world as props in numerous movies. Shortly after Henry Huntington purchased LARY in 1898, his engineers designed a standard car for Los Angeles' balmy climate. A distinctive five-window front and wire mesh side enclosures were placed on the ends of a closed center section car and the "Huntington Standard" was created. In a city so dependent on the jet age, the total number of Standards is ironic — 747. Though some were rebuilt pre-Huntington cars, most of the Standards were newly built between 1902 and 1912. Rebuilt with wood side panels and interior amenities, some of these cars served until 1952. Still serviceable in its 41st year, car 421 is on the Griffith Shuttle just prior to its abandonment on June 30, 1946. — *Robert T. McVay*

During 1912, LARY's riders demanded a low step car, a demand in part the result of hobble skirt fashions. Thus, 76 center-entrance cars were built by St. Louis Car Co. LARY also had ambitious, but perhaps misguided, plans to rebuild all 747 Standards by inserting a 7′6″ low-floor section into the center of the car. By 1914, 107 Standards were rebuilt when the program was stopped due to revenue losses to jitney competition. Fortu-

nately, the rebuildings did not resume as subsequent economic conditions dictated one-man operation; whereas, these cars required two men. These unique cars, whose design led to their nickname, "sowbellies", survived until 1947. One of the four-motor variety, car 73, rebuilt from Standard car 281, lumbers westward on Temple Street near Edgeware on an "A" line run in the summer of 1946. — *Robert T. McVay*

A quiet corner in the Eagle Rock district is shared by two generations of surface transit vehicles. The 1946-vintage GM bus is on a Route 25 North Fugueroa-West Ninth schedule. Car 1400 is one of 250 type-H steel body, California-style, two-man, multiple-unit cars built by St. Louis Car Co. between 1920 and 1923. Regular train operation ended in 1930, and by 1936, the first 215 cars, 1201-1415, had been rebuilt for one-man service.

The last 35 cars, 1416-1450, were rebuilt with their open sections enclosed and upholstered leather seats as "deluxe cars" for suburban routes like Line 5, the 21-mile Eagle Rock/Hawthorne route. When car 1400 leaves Eagle Rock Boulevard and Colorado Boulevard, in Los Angeles' northeast corner, it will travel over extensive private rights-of-way through downtown to Hawthorne in the city's southwest section. — *Donald Duke*

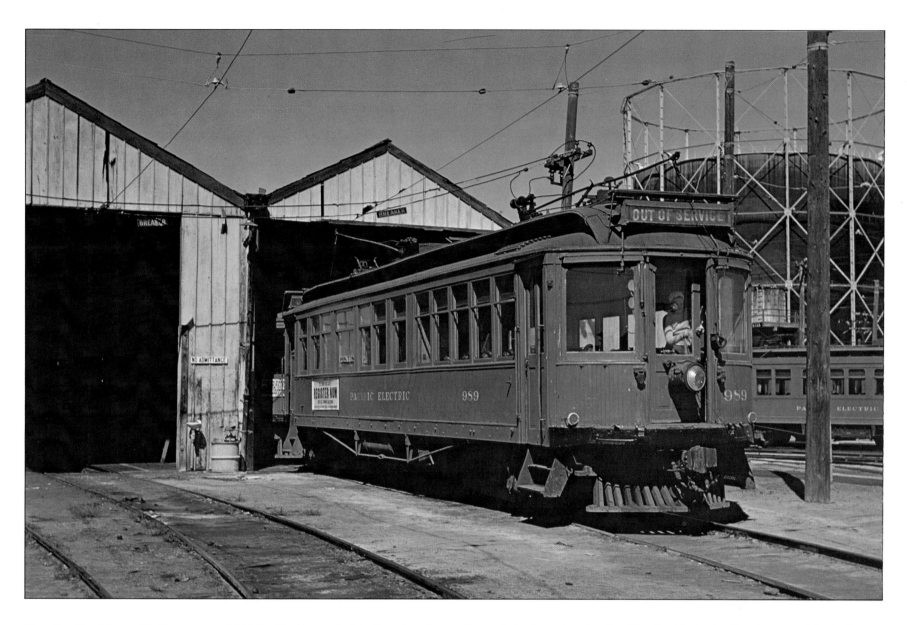

Shortly after Moses H. Sherman and Eli P. Clark's arrival in Los Angeles in 1890, they began to acquire street railways. By 1898, their properties had been reorganized as LARY, and on October 1, 1898, LARY was sold to Henry E. Huntington and Isaias W. Hellman. Thereafter, all of these men devoted their efforts to interurban lines. Huntington and Hellman formed the Pacific Electric in 1901, three years after Sherman and Clark formed the Los Angeles Pacific. In 1906, the Southern Pacific Railroad gained control of LAP and acquired 50% of the PE's common stock. In 1908, the fifty 700-series cars were purchased. In 1924, car 739 became 989 and it returned to serve former LAP lines, now PE's Western District, after 13 years in Pasadena service. Two years before its retirement, 989 is at Ocean Park carhouse, Venice in February 1948. — *George Krambles*

Huntington long expected to be SP's president. However, in 1901, when it became evident that this was not to be, he formed the PE. Soon Hellman could no longer support Huntington's spending, so he sold his interests in LARY and PE to the SP. With control of LAP, E. H. Harriman pressed Huntington and in 1910, SP acquired his PE stock in exchange for SP's LARY stock plus cash. Thereafter, SP acted to modernize and upgrade PE. In 1913, Jewett delivered 45 cars of the 1000-series, which entered service immediately as trailers for the summer rush to Long Beach. Through that fall and into 1914, they were shopped to receive motors and control equipment. On July 23, 1949, 1019 leads 1052 and 1033 on a Santa Anita Race Track Special near the track on the Monrovia-Glendora line, one of many special services provided by PE. — *John E. Koschwanez*

Certainly no one can fault SP's management of the PE in the decade after the 1911 merger. Extensive car purchases, significant route extensions and several other improvements were made. Car 1217, at 6th and Main on July 1, 1947, typifies the PE of that era. PE sought to modernize equipment on the long run over its new line to San Bernadino. The arrival of cars 1200 to 1221 in 1915 marked the pinnacle of PE car design but one must ques-tion if they were used to their full potential. The premier "Citrus Belt Limited" of 1922 could manage only a 33 mph average on the 57-mile Los Angeles-San Bernardino run. By 1937, the 1200's were averaging 31.5 mph on the L.A.-Baldwin Park portion of the "San Berdoo" line. When the line was cut back to Baldwin Park in 1947, this had deteriorated to a 51 minute schedule to cover those 18 miles. — *Robert T. McVay*

A system of PE's size, which as late as 1945 used 2260 pieces of rolling stock and employed 7,100 people, required substantial support facilities. The greatest of these facilities, Torrance Shops, opened in 1918, on a 61-acre tract in the city of Torrance, which is near San Pedro. The shops' capabilities for major overhauls and rebuildings are well-illustrated by the changes to the "Hollywood" class cars. Car 630, one of 160 suburban cars, was built by St. Louis Car Co. in 1922. By 1938, public pressure forced PE to substantially upgrade the series. By 1949, economic pressures demanded one-man operation and 630 became 5119. On December 26, 1952, two days before service to the San Fernando Valley ended, 5119 is stopping at Rio Vista. Reassigned to Watts service, car 5119 became LAMTA 1808 in 1958 and was scrapped in 1959. — *Donald Duke*

Los Angeles' wide-spread development resulted in a low population density which, when combined with the early dependence on automobiles, placed PE in a precarious position. Following the Depression, antiquated cars and neglected physical plant dictated a substantial financial commitment to retain rail service. For the Glendale-Burbank line PE chose, effective July 12, 1936, to substitute buses for most off-peak trains. By 1939, it was evident that buses were no substitute for the private right-of-way and subway rail route. PE was ordered to reinstate full rail service utilizing modern equipment, which was done by November 24, 1940. Two of the 30 double end, MU PCC's which arrived in 1940, are on the high bridge over Fletcher Drive on June 2, 1951, just 4 years before Metropolitan Coach Lines abandoned the rail route. — *George Krambles*

PE conducted significant freight operations. Carloads of citrus, oil and general merchandise were moved in great numbers on the San Pedro, San Bernardino and El Segundo lines and in less numbers on virtually all lines except those to Hollywood and Pasadena. PE also maintained a large fleet of box motors to haul less-than-carload freight, mail and express. RPO cars operated from 1905 until May 6, 1950, when service to San Bernar-dino, the last trolley RPO which started at an incredible late date of September 2, 1947, made its last run. On October 28, 1952, motor 1463 is at Los Nietos on the Whittier line. This motor, rebuilt from an ex-Portland car in 1941, though capable of pulling several cars, was limited to one by a full crew law. LCL services ended on November 15, 1952, while carloads operations continue in 1978 as part of the SP. — *Donald Duke*

PE had a most visible terminal spiral of deferring maintenance and deteriorating service. In fairness to PE, SP's interest flagged after traffic volumes declined in the early 1920's. However, as other SP electrified operations were abandoned, SP reassigned many cars to PE's fleet. From Northwestern Pacific and Interurban Electric, both San Francisco commuter operations, came the famous "Blimps." The first of these 73-foot cars were leased from SP in 1942 to meet World War II traffic surges. In September 1952, PE 318, ex-PE 4506, ex-NWP leads a Santa Catalina Boat (connecting) train into San Pedro Street behind the 6th & Main Los Angeles terminal. These cars carried PE's last rail passengers in 1961. Three of them together with other PE and LARY equipment, are preserved at the Orange Empire Trolley Museum. — *George Krambles*

In the late 1940's storm clouds were gathering. From an economic perspective, PE's continuing losses precluded improvements. However, Los Angeles' failure to preserve a significant social asset is hard to explain in light of numerous incredibly expensive proposed rapid transit systems that will only partially replace the "Big Red Cars." In reprise, we present PE 999. *Old Flat Front,* built in 1907 as LAP 747, was rebuilt, in 1909, as deluxe private car *El Viento* (The Wind). Conveyed to PE in 1911, it was rebuilt into Office Car 01, renumbered as 999, and rebuilt in 1929 for regular service. Though assigned to the Venice Short Line until its abandonment on September 17, 1950, special duties continued, like this 1947 fantrip at Eaton Wash Bridge, Sierra Madre. It certainly has been fun to *Remember When . . . — George Krambles*